# GLUTEN FREE, NATURALLY

*101 gorgeous
recipes to transform
the way you eat*

## CAROLINE BYRON

# GLUTEN FREE, NATURALLY

PHOTOGRAPHY BY CLARE WINFIELD

KYLE BOOKS

For Alan.

Published in 2018 by Kyle Books
www.kylebooks.com

Distributed by National Book Network
4501 Forbes Blvd, Suite 200,
Lanham, MD 20706
Phone: (800) 462-6420
Fax: (800) 338-4550
customercare@nbnbooks.com

First published in Great Britain in 2018 by
Kyle Books, an imprint of Octopus Publishing
Group Ltd.

10 9 8 7 6 5 4 3 2 1

ISBN 978-1-909487-84-0

Project Editor: Tara O'Sullivan
Editorial Assistant: Sarah Kyle
Editorial Adaptation: Christopher Steighner
Designer: Abi Hartshorne
Photographer: Clare Winfield
Food Stylist: Annie Rigg
Prop Stylist: Polly Webb-Wilson
Production: Nic Jones and Gemma John

Library of Congress Control Number: 2017963601

Color reproduction by ALTA London
Printed and bound in China by C&C Offset
Printing Co., Ltd.

# CONTENTS

# INTRODUCTION

I have been eating gluten-free food on and off since the age of 14, and I cannot emphasize enough the positive impact it has had on my life. In the years since, my health has improved immeasurably, and I have spent many enjoyable hours in my kitchen developing the recipes that I'm now sharing with you.

There is, of course, a lot of debate over gluten free—is it a fad or a fact? All I can tell you is that when I removed the gluten from my diet, many of the health issues I was suffering from disappeared. Going gluten free has helped me, and while it may not be for everyone, it's a lifestyle choice that I, along with many millions of people around the world, have chosen and will continue to follow.

If you have picked up this book, it's likely that you are considering adopting, or already follow, a gluten-free lifestyle. Whether you are gluten intolerant or celiac, or you are just looking to cook for a friend or family member who is, or, perhaps, you have Lyme disease, like I did, I hope that my journey might inspire you to try going gluten free and show you that you don't need to deprive yourself of your favorite foods to do so.

The the recipes and ideas in this book are all about offering a third way: the "happy middle" of cooking delicious, satisfying food that also happens to be gluten-free. Life is not black and white. I want to show that there is a way where we can all still have a little of what we love—a little bit of indulgence—but combined with the things that we know are good for us. I know everyone seems to be "free from" something at the moment when it comes to food—but you know the main thing I am free from? Guilt. And I want you to be guilt-free too—even when you eat my amazing gluten-free fried chicken!

This book is about forgiveness, great food, and, of course, having fun eating it and cooking it. I call it "guilt-free living." So forgive yourself and be healthy—but don't make food a stick to beat yourself with!

Caroline xxx

# HOW I CAME TO BE
# GLUTEN FREE

I recently moved to London to study nutrition. But in a previous life I was a model in New York, after which I trained in classical French cuisine—a slightly unusual career change but it made perfect sense to me at the time, as I hated modeling and have always loved eating!

As you'll see on page 12—Lyme Disease and Me—I was first introduced to gluten free back in my teens when it was one of the things that helped me with the effects of my illness. However, like most teenagers, I abandoned the healthy lifestyle when I got better and almost forgot about it. A few years later, when I left the world of modeling, where everything was eaten on the run—if anything was eaten at all—and I lived instead on a diet of sandwiches and sodas, I decided to return to my first love, and so I trained in French cuisine at the French Culinary Institute in New York (now known as the International Culinary Centre). I learned how to cook from the French masters, and so began a magical adventure in food—from deep smoky bouillabaisses to the silky gravy of the perfect coq au vin and, of course, all that yummy patisserie. I lived the whole, "Oui, Chef! Non, Chef!" lifestyle. I was learning so much and I absolutely loved it! However, as well as learning to cook, I also learned to eat with a typical Gallic abandon and excess. All those delicious hot, buttery creations; all that rich pastry, cream, and sugar; the eclairs, macarons, petit fours—they all had to be tested, didn't they?

But as the quantities of delicious gluten increased, so too did my weight. I was having terrible problems with my gut, my skin was out of control, my mood was all over the place, and my sleep was erratic. This very high-gluten, classic French diet led me to discover I was gluten intolerant. Frustratingly, no sooner had I mastered the entire French culinary repertoire, than I found I couldn't actually eat any of it!

When I left culinary school, I knew I had to make a change because my health was so terrible—almost as bad as it had been in my teenage years. Initially, I began to wean myself off sugar, replacing that oh-so-addictive stuff with Medjool dates and raw cacao. I started a course of Vitamin A for my skin. I began doing hot yoga three or four times a week and I went to vegan restaurants in New York's West Village, where the yoga studio was. I researched everything that went into or onto my body.

Then I remembered the gluten-free diet that my doctor and naturopath had prescribed me when I was very sick as a kid. So I began to retrace my steps and, once again, as an adult I cut out all the sources of traditional gluten: breads, cakes, pasta—all the things that I loved in life. Within weeks, my skin cleared up, my mood stabilized, I stopped feeling bloated all the time, and I was getting good, restorative sleep.

I began to look at what I put in my body and its relationship to what was happening with my skin and my general wellbeing. I investigated all the new ideas and theories about food and its relationship with the gut and skin. Our skin is a mirror for what is happening inside our bodies: our food intake, our hydration—it all shows on the surface. When travelling to Europe, I would stick to salads; when shopping, I went almost exclusively for vegetables and fruit—all of which was great, and my diet today is still biased towards those things. But as much as I was enjoying being healthy again and looking and feeling great—both inside and out—I missed the foods I loved so much. I was really starting to crave my beloved baked goods!

The taste of warm freshly baked bread in the morning with butter is a delight that I for one was not about to give up on for good. The difficult part was how to translate the rich, brown crusty loaves that we made in school into no-gluten recipes that tasted as good. How could I recreate those soft, fudgy chocolate brownies that I had cooked from childhood? And how was it possible to make crumbly cookies or moist juicy cakes or even my favorite pesto and pasta dishes that I had learned to love so much on my travels to Italy?

I was determined not to give up the food I loved. So it was time to learn to cook again from scratch and re-teach myself with a whole new pantry of ingredients—to understand how the flours all worked together and how taking the gluten (and therefore the elasticity) out of recipes had to be compensated for with new ideas—but never sacrificing on either the flavor or texture. If I want a gooey chocolate dessert at the end of a meal, I really don't want it to be made from an avocado—it's just not the same thing at all. I wanted recipes that taste as good as the originals—food that makes you go "yum!" and gives you the warm feeling of satisfaction that only good food can bring.

When I first went gluten free there was nowhere for me to go to learn how to cook for and stick with a gluten-free life. I just had to teach myself. I took all my old recipe books back to the kitchen and adapted them, one by one, to create gluten-free versions. Pizza, cakes, breads, and cookies—I reworked them all and came up with my own recipes for the perfect gluten-free flour mixes with sorghum, millet, almond, G-F oat flour, and many more. And I worked out alternatives to dairy and to sugar wherever possible.

I spent an entire summer experimenting with gluten-free pastry alone and working on new ideas to prove to myself that I could eat gluten free and still have all the foods that I missed—and not some poor imitation that fell apart in my hand or was as hard as a rock to bite into! There are some recipes in here that are everyday go-tos, but there are also some more complicated ones, like my light-as-air choux pastry for my sweet chocolate eclairs—firm on the outside, soft and gooey on the inside—or my gluten-free puff pastry. Give them a try. They may seem daunting at first, but with a little trial and error (and a few spare afternoons to practice!), you may just surprise yourself and see how easy even advanced gluten-free baking can be. And note that gluten-free baked goods do not last well—if you cook from fresh, then you will need to eat everything up within 24 hours. That's an order!

The one thing that I have to admit I have not yet managed to make is a perfect gluten-free French croissant. I just cannot get the texture right and I have yet to taste one that works. (I have often been asked what would make me break my gluten-free diet and I have to say it would be a croissant dipped into my morning coffee; but sadly, even just one croissant affects my gut and my mood so badly I have to stay away.)

Going gluten free means knowing how to shop as well as cook. Because gluten-free food has less elasticity and fewer preservatives than standard baked goods, you will find some great ready-made gluten-free foods in the freezer section as they keep much better that way. I often buy frozen gluten-free bread if I don't have time to bake from scratch (but if you do have time, there are lots of recipes in this book for breads such as crusty baguettes and focaccia).

I have radically changed my life by educating myself about food and cooking and eating and adapting to a gluten-free lifestyle and I know that it has made me feel better, which is why I believe I have something to share. I am in control of my life and my kitchen and am so much more at ease with myself and my body now than ever before.

I hope my experience and my recipes will make being gluten-free a little easier for you. Cooking is all about taking back control over your diet and your life. And, as with so many things, it's about getting the right balance. Gluten free isn't for everyone, but if it is for you, or a family member, then join me on this journey. After all, just because you are gluten free, it doesn't mean you have to miss out.

## MY KITCHEN MUST-HAVES

I have been building my kitchen for years. My kitchen gadgets are more precious to me than any handbag! Of course, my Vitamix is my closest partner—it's so easy to use for soups, smoothies, and remedies. I really recommend investing in a good blender. And I love my Kuvings juicer. It gives cold-pressed juice for the best results. I also use a Cuisinart food processor and a KitchenAid mixer as well as a KitchenAid ice-cream and yogurt maker.

My most used everyday tools are my food mill, sieve, and Salter scales.

I also suggest investing in some good knives. My favorite brands are Wusthof, Global, Kai Shun, and MAC.

For my baking hardware I tend to use Gobel tins and molds, as well as classic French baking utensils for more interesting shapes.

My saucepans are a mixture—mainly Mauviel, Staub, SKK, and, of course, my beloved bright blue Le Creuset.

# LYME DISEASE AND ME

Sadly, Lyme disease has been one of the formative influences of my life.

When I was 10, my family left New York and moved to Connecticut to a really, really small town called Weston, about an hour and a half's drive from New York City.

Unfortunately, very soon after I got sick—really sick. No one knew what was causing all my gastric and neurological symptoms, complete exhaustion, painful joints and so on. Well, it turned out it was Lyme disease, but because I didn't have the classic bull's-eye rash associated with the disease, it took over a year until I was diagnosed and by that point I was very ill. Lyme disease is a bacterial infection carried by spider-like ticks living in areas of woodland (or, in this case, my dad's golf course). It's actually named after Lyme, Connecticut, only 60 miles from Weston and where the first case was diagnosed in the 1970s. I was unlucky because if you diagnose and treat the illness right away, it'll be out of your system with just a few weeks of antibiotics, but in my case it spread throughout my body and brain, so no two-week course of antibiotics was going to get rid of it.

I was ill for eight years. I was exhausted all the time, had terrible migraines, my balance was affected, and I had neurological symptoms. I was fortunate in that a lot of people get arthritis with the disease, whereas I just had muscular pain. Then there were also the side effects of the treatments, which were pretty debilitating as well. When I was 14, I had six months of intravenous antibiotics therapy, which was not great for my gut! And when that didn't work, my parents decided to go down a more holistic route, so I was sent to do hyperbaric oxygen treatment at an oxygen chamber center in Massachusetts for six months. This involves being put into a highly pressurized chamber pumped full of oxygen for an hour a day. It's a bizarre experience, to say the least. Bizarre and slightly nightmarish—and weird too, because you're in this chamber with other people. (The single chambers were really claustrophobic, so I opted for the bigger chamber which is shared with three or four other people, so at least there is more space.)

I can't really say if the oxygen treatment helped or not because immediately afterwards I went to a naturopath who suggested a gluten-free diet. At the time, research was just beginning to show a correlation between Lyme disease and gluten intolerance—something which many Lyme sufferers have noticed, although studies are still in their very early stages.

Back then, gluten free was considered a bit hippy-dippy. Few brands produced gluten-free foods or ingredients and so we had to learn the hard way. But I went gluten free for six months and I started to feel a whole lot better. It was a lot of work though—I was gluten free a decade before the rest of the world caught on and made it a little easier!

As a result of my Lyme disease, I was home schooled, as I was just too sick to leave the house on most days, and I also had to give up my favorite physical activities, from tennis to ballet. And so food filled the void, and cooking, especially baking, became my first big hobby. My Raspberry Almond Shortbread Cookies were my first recipe, which is still one of my most treasured (see page 129 for the now gluten-free version). At first, I burned more than I baked... but as I got more confident and I realized my family actually enjoyed eating what I gave them, I moved on to more complicated recipes.

By the time I was a teenager, I had claimed our family kitchen as my own. While other girls my age were reading Judy Blume and dancing to Spice Girls videos on MTV, I already had my subscription to *Bon Appétit* magazine and was hooked on Food Network. (Who needs Posh Spice when you have Ina Garten, the Barefoot Contessa—still, to this day, my total idol!) Along with my darling Nana, she and domestic goddess Nigella Lawson got me through those years; them and the love of making delicious food for myself and my family. Until, that is, a lot of my favorite recipes became redundant because I could no longer eat gluten—and it would be a decade before I worked out how to recreate them.

By the time I was 18, I was starting to feel a lot better, which I put down to going gluten free. The Lyme was on its way out, so I said, "OK… I'm done with that!" and returned to eating gluten. However, as I explained in my introduction, when I was training in classical French cuisine in my 20s and gorging on beautiful patisserie and gluten-rich sauces all day, I once again started feeling really sick—and that's what brought me back to gluten free.

I have never been tested for coeliac, which would involve an endoscopy and a biopsy, but I am certainly sensitive to gluten—even a tiny amount eaten in error is enough to make my skin break out and bring back the mood swings that plagued my teenage years.

Doctors tell me that some of the symptoms of Lyme are similar to some of those of celiac disease: fatigue, muscle and joint pain, peripheral neuropathy or numbness, and tingling and cognitive impairment, including brain fog. And I know that many, many Lyme sufferers have found that going gluten free can have a beneficial effect on their symptoms. So if you are a sufferer from this debilitating infection, which is becoming increasingly common in the the US, all I can say is perhaps give gluten free a try. After all, it's a lot easier now than it was when I was 15. And, unlike me, you won't have to go to the trouble of working out how to make all your favorite recipes gluten free—because I've already done that for you!

# GLUTEN-FREE FLOURS

For those new to baking gluten free, or to baking in general, it can be a daunting prospect. The gluten-free baking section at Whole Foods has more than 50 different flours or mixes. And while it's great that so many gluten-free options are available, it can be intimidating and difficult to know what to choose, especially with so many of the flours and gums having weird, unfamiliar names: xanthan gum, sorghum, amaranth, teff...

I knew next to nothing about these ingredients or how they worked when I got started with gluten-free baking, but through a bit of research and lots of trial and error, I got a sense of what ratios and combinations worked to achieve flavors and textures as good as the classic wheat-based equivalents.

There are lots of all-purpose gluten-free flour blends out there now, and while some of them work well for certain recipes, they don't cut it for others. Many of these blends use cheaper flours, which give the final product an inferior texture or a weird flavor (I'm talking about chickpea or bean flours here). So although it is a bit more time consuming, I've always had much better luck making and using my own individual blends. And if you're going to put the time and money into gluten-free baking, you might as well do it right and make cookies that taste like cookies, not beans.

Having said that, there are a few high-quality gluten-free flour blends on the market. The ones I favor are Cup 4 Cup and Pamela's gluten-free blend. However, they do tend to be expensive and I find mixing my own blends a better option for most recipes.

The biggest challenge to getting started with gluten-free baking is understanding how to replace traditional all-purpose wheat flour. Unfortunately, no one ingredient is going to do it. To achieve the texture, flavor, and binding of wheat flour calls for at least three different gluten-free flours, sometimes more. For most baked goods that combination is:

- **A fine, mild base flour – my favorite is sorghum, but rice flours can also work.**

- **A starch to give lightness – either tapioca or potato and cornstarch, as a rule.**

- **A denser, heavier whole-grain flour for flavor and texture – almond, oat, or millet.**

The ratio of these three varies, based on the desired texture. I personally lean towards blends that include more of the earthier flours like sorghum and buckwheat, but for very delicate pastries and cakes requiring a fine crumb, more starch and rice flour are generally needed.

The following pages give a brief overview of all of the flours I use in my baking.

## SORGHUM FLOUR

My favorite base flour for pretty much any recipe, sorghum has a smooth texture and mild, sweet taste. It is often labelled "Sweet" White Sorghum Flour because of its subtle flavor and light color. Despite being relatively unknown, it's the third-biggest cereal crop in the US and fifth in the world. Sorghum also has tons of nutritional benefits—it's high in protein, iron, fiber, and antioxidants. It is also non-genetically modified (non-GMO).

## MILLET FLOUR

Made from ground millet (most commonly known as birdseed in the US), this is the sixth-most important grain in the world. It's also super healthy, being high in magnesium and antioxidants, and it's been found helpful in controling diabetes and inflammation. Millet flour is yellow in color with a light texture and sweet, nutty flavor that works really well in breads and muffins and cakes. Millet is a fantastic secondary flour to give layered flavor and a nutritional boost.

## ALMOND FLOUR

Made simply from ground almonds, this is one of my favorite ingredients. It is high in protein, low in carbs, and has a very low glycemic index (GI). This means it won't spike your blood sugar, making it one of the healthiest gluten-free flours. It gives a great chewy texture to baked goods and a wonderful nutty, sweet flavor. It is best used as a secondary flour (about 25 per cent of the mix) because it is very dense and has a high fat content.

## HAZELNUT FLOUR

This is made from ground hazelnuts and generally interchangeable with almond flour. You can make your own at home by grinding blanched or peeled hazelnuts until fine in a food processor or dry Vitamix/blender.

## BUCKWHEAT FLOUR

Made from ground buckwheat, which, despite its name, is not related to wheat at all and is actually a fruit in the rhubarb family. Buckwheat flour is dark in color and adds a distinctive tone and flavor in baking. It is high in protein and fiber and has a nut-like flavor. I love using it in traditional ways like buckwheat crêpes or blinis, but it's also great in moderation in other earthier or savory recipes.

## TEFF FLOUR

I had never heard of teff before going gluten free, but it's a tiny ancient grain that has been a staple in northeast Africa for centuries and is the smallest grain in the world. Teff flour—made from ground teff—is caramel in color with a lovely nutty flavor and light texture. It's also a great source of calcium, protein, and iron. I love using it in breads and muffins, where it adds a subtle sweetness and an almost cake-like texture. Use for 25 to 50 per cent of total flour in recipes.

## BROWN RICE FLOUR

This is a staple base flour in gluten-free baking. It is extremely versatile and can be used in sweet or savory products. Rice flours can often have a gritty texture, so finding a finely ground brown rice flour is important—my favorites are Bob's Red Mill or Authentic Foods, who make a superfine version that is great for pastry. However, because there are some concerns over the arsenic content in brown rice, I tend to go for other gluten-free flours, despite the versatility of brown rice flour. If you can't find sorghum or gluten-free oat flour though, brown rice flour is a great 1:1 substitute.

## WHITE RICE FLOUR

A staple base flour made from white rice that can generally be substituted for brown rice flour. Because of its light color and texture, it is very useful in fine pastries, white breads, and delicate crumb cakes. You generally find this rice flour in most commercial gluten-free flour mixes due to its versatility.

## SWEET RICE FLOUR

Despite also being known as glutinous rice flour, this flour is entirely gluten free. It is a bit confusingly named and can also be labelled as Mochiko, based on the Japanese name for the glutinous rice it is made from and the name by which it is referred to in Asia. Made from Japanese sticky rice, it is very starchy and binding. Used in moderation, it gives a great, springy texture to muffins, breads, doughnuts, and more. It is also great for giving durability to dough that needs to be rolled out, like tart crusts.

## GLUTEN-FREE OAT FLOUR

Some people who are gluten intolerant or have celiac disease are sensitive to oats, even if they have been processed in a gluten-free facility and are not contaminated. So for many people gluten-free oats and the flour made from them are a great option. Gluten-free oat flour is very light and soft in texture and is a great base flour when mixed with heavier ones like almond, millet or quinoa to give it texture and density. It is great in cookies and cakes.

## QUINOA FLOUR

Made from ground quinoa, this is a great way to add protein and flavor to your baking. It can have a strong flavor if used as a base flour and can make items too crumbly, however, so it is best used sparingly.

## TAPIOCA STARCH

Also known as tapioca flour and one of the most commonly used ingredients in gluten-free baking, this is made from the starch extracted from the South American cassava plant. Tapioca starch is essentially just the ground version of the tapioca pearls used in desserts. It is essentially flavorless with no nutritional value, but it gives structure to gluten-free baked goods and helps them achieve a golden brown color and crisp texture.

## POTATO STARCH

Made from the starch from crushed potatoes, this should not be confused with potato flour. Potato starch is the refined starch extracted from potatoes and is always pure white, whereas potato flour is a heavy, yellowish flour made by crushing and dehydrating whole cooked potatoes. Potato flour retains a strong potato flavour and is not at all interchangeable with the light, flavourless potato starch.

## CORNSTARCH

This is the starch derived from corn and is very useful in gluten-free baking and cooking. It can take the place of traditional wheat flour for thickening sauces or breading chicken and has many uses in baked goods. It has a very light texture and is particularly good in delicate cakes and some breads. It is similar to but more versatile than potato and tapioca starch. And because corn is a gluten-free grain, there are many products made from it that are useful in gluten-free cooking but can be somewhat tricky to differentiate due to the different names they are given. Even though they all come from corn, they cannot be substituted for each other and behave very differently.

**Corn flour** is a label for extremely finely ground cornmeal used specifically for baking things like cornbread.

**Cornmeal/polenta** is the simplest of corn products, as it is just dried corn that has been ground to varying degrees of fineness. Cornmeal is very common in America, where it is generally produced from dent (or field) corn and finely milled with steel rollers. In Europe it is less common and traditional polenta from Italy is milled from flint corn and similar in texture to medium-grind cornmeal. Most other non-Italian polentas are produced from dent corn. If you can't find cornmeal, you can generally substitute polenta—non-Italian, preferably—but you may end up with a bit more texture.

**Masa harina.** "Masa harina" means "dough flour" in Spanish, and this is the traditional flour used to make tortillas and tamales. Very different from any other of the previous corn products, masa harina is made from ground hominy (corn kernels that have been soaked in slaked lime to remove the hulls).

## ARROWROOT

A starch derived from tropical plants, arrowroot is commonly used in Asian cuisine. In addition to lightening gluten-free baked goods, it's great for thickening sauces. Other thickeners like cornstarch make sauces cloudy, whereas sauces thickened with arrowroot are clear. It also has some non-baking uses. Traditionally, tea made from boiling the root alone is amazing for your skin. Finding the plant itself is difficult, although some Asian markets carry it, but I find a homemade mask made from the starch and topically applied is very smoothing and calming for the skin. It is one of my favorite home remedies.

## LEAVENING

**Baking powder** is a mixture of a baking soda and Cream of Tartar, which increases the volume and lightens baked goods—especially cakes. Baking powder works by releasing carbon dioxide into the batter, causing bubbles to expand and thus leavening the mixture. Baking powder is naturally gluten free, but starch is used as a filler in this product. Most baking powders use cornstarch but it's best to check that it is not wheat starch.

**Baking soda** is an alkali. It needs an acid and a liquid to activate it. You will usually find a recipe containing baking soda also calls for something like cream of tartar, yogurt, buttermilk, or milk. Like baking powder, baking soda releases carbon dioxide when activated. Once cooked, the carbon dioxide is replaced by air, which lightens your baking. This is naturally gluten free.

**Cream of tartar** is technically called tartaric acid, an acid and a by-product of wine production. Most often used with baking soda, it produces carbon dioxide. It stabilizes egg whites and can also stop sugar syrup from crystalizing. This is naturally gluten free.

**Active dried yeast** is the most common yeast used in bread making and needs to be dissolved in warm water, with a pinch of sugar to feed it. Instant yeast is a more rapid yeast — you use much less than active yeast and you can add straight to the flour. These are naturally gluten free.

# FEEDING THE FEW

## QUICK AND EASY DISHES

Some of my most cherished recipes are those I make for my closest friends when there are just a few of us to feed. The day I got the keys to my first apartment I hosted an impromptu dinner party for my four closest friends: Akbar and his boyfriend, Stephen, Sanga, and my crazy British friend Richard. The first things I unpacked were my beloved Le Creuset saucepans and my Wüsthof knives, which I've had since culinary school. I had six plates, three glasses, two mugs, and assorted cutlery. I stepped out to Whole Foods and grabbed a huge bunch of fresh basil, some lush dark green lacinato kale, a hunk of Italian Parmesan, some zesty fresh lemons, some beautiful tomatoes and some dried pasta. A bottle (or two) of wine was opened to celebrate, and we christened my new kitchen. I remember that kitchen supper so clearly, as we all sat on the floor, each with a bowl brimming over with my creamy Genovese pesto and pasta, scattered with little pieces of sweet yellow and red heirloom tomatoes.

This is the section of the book that will become, I hope, your everyday go-to for gluten-free cooking. At the heart of all good cooking are the basics, and when you go gluten free, there are so many standard recipes you have to amend—things you totally forgot had flour in them, like gravy. I have given you my stock recipes, as well as a variety of gravies that should cover most dishes, from classic gravy to a red wine or cider version and a pepper gravy, perfect for steaks (see page 39).

When I cook for myself, I tend to favor salads or soups. For salads, I love to combine earthy flavors like beet or kale with fruity and zesty partners like pomegranate or orange. So I hope these will become your go-to salads. Equally, for soups, I have included some summer soups, like the fabulous cold Spanish Ajo Blanco (see page 42) and my failsafe cold remedy for the winter months, Warming Chicken, Ginger, and Rice Soup (see page 40).

As well as a good selection of flours (see page 14), your gluten-free larder should also always be well stocked with a good assortment of dried pasta. I have recipes for fresh pasta in other sections, but one of my favorite pasta dishes in the world is Spaghetti alla Nerano (see p. 58), which I make with store-bought spaghetti. For an easy mid-week meal, gluten-free dried pasta can be a life saver.

# COCONUT CHIA PUDDING

## WITH FRESH STRAWBERRY PURÉE AND CRUNCHY GRANOLA

This dish is fantastic when you're in a rush in the morning, as it can all be made ahead. It's my absolute go-to recipe; not only is it incredibly tasty, but the chia seeds are packed with antioxidants, fiber, fatty acids, and calcium. You can keep the chia pudding and purée in your refrigerator overnight and the granola will keep for several weeks in an airtight container. The strawberry purée can also be refrigerated and gives an instant dash of color and blast of fruitiness, while the granola gives you the crunch and a sense of depth and warmth to keep you going until lunch.

## SERVES 4

### FOR THE COCONUT CHIA PUDDING
1 cup coconut milk
1 teaspoon vanilla extract
3 tablespoons chia seeds

### FOR THE STRAWBERRY PURÉE
1 cup fresh strawberries, chopped into similar-sized pieces
1 to 2 teaspoons coconut sugar (optional, to taste)

### FOR THE GRANOLA
(MAKES 15 SERVINGS)
2 cups whole rolled oats
½ cup nuts (almonds or unsalted cashews)
½ cup seeds (sesame, sunflower, pumpkin)
¼ cup coconut flakes
1 tablespoon coconut oil, melted
2 tablespoons honey
1 tablespoon maple syrup
1 teaspoon vanilla extract
½ cup unsweetened chopped dried fruit (cranberries, cherries, raisins, apricots)
pinch of sea salt

**To make the coconut chia pudding,** mix all the ingredients, then cook over a medium heat for 2 minutes to warm slightly. Cover and refrigerate overnight.

**For the strawberry purée,** place the strawberries and sugar in a heavy-based saucepan and cook over a gentle heat for 5 to 7 minutes. Lower the heat if the sugar and berries seem to be sticking; you want the sugar to dissolve, the juices to be released, and the fruit to begin to break down. Cool and blend in food processor. Strain with a sieve, pressing down with the back of a spoon to extract all the precious juice. Cover and refrigerate.

**Next, make the granola.** Preheat the oven to 325°F.

Place the oats, nuts, seeds, and coconut flakes in a bowl.

Heat the coconut oil, honey, maple syrup, and vanilla extract gently in a small pan until combined. Pour the liquid over the dry ingredients and stir to coat.

Spread onto a baking sheet and level. Bake for about 15 to 20 mintes until golden brown. Keep an eye on the granola and stir to stop it darkening too much around the edges.

Once cool, stir in the dried fruit. This will keep for up to 3 weeks in an airtight container.

Serve all three components chilled together in a serving bowl.

# BANANA SYRUP BUCKWHEAT GRIDDLE CAKES

The banana is really the mother of all superfoods. As well as being an amazing source of potassium, it's also like a multivitamin supplement—and, of course, it's entirely portable. I usually grab a banana if I'm going to the gym in the morning, but this recipe is the best for a lazy Saturday morning brunch. You can use an egg replacer for a vegan version and coconut milk instead of buttermilk, if you wish—it all works. The caramelized banana and nuts give this dish extra bite.

## MAKES 12

¾ cup buckwheat flour

¼ cup sorghum flour

¼ cup oat flour

¼ cup cornmeal

1 teaspoon gluten-free baking powder

1 large free-range egg

1 cup and 2 tablespoons buttermilk (1 cup of milk with the juice of 1 small lemon) or coconut milk

1 tablespoon coconut oil, melted, plus extra for frying

3 bananas

4 teaspoons maple syrup, plus extra for drizzling

¼ cup unsalted nuts (almonds, cashews, pistachios)

Mix the flours, cornmeal, and baking powder together in a large bowl.

In a pitcher, whisk the egg, buttermilk (or coconut milk), and coconut oil.

Make a well in the center of the flours and whisk in the egg and milk mixture, so you have a smooth batter.

Mash one of the bananas and fold into the batter mixture.

Heat a heavy-based large frying pan over a medium-high heat, add a teaspoon of coconut oil, then add generous tablespoons of the batter mix to make each griddle cake. You will need to cook them in batches.

Once all the griddle cakes are cooked, keep them warm in a low oven while you prepare the bananas.

Slice the remaining bananas and cook over a low-medium heat in 1 to 2 teaspoons of coconut oil and the maple syrup, until caramelized.

Serve the griddle cakes with the nuts, caramelized banana, and an extra drizzle of maple syrup.

# BERRY OATMEAL BREAKFAST COBBLER

This is a great dish that can be eaten hot or cold—so it's perfect if you need to take your breakfast out on the road with you, eat after an exercise class, or after the school run, for instance. Just stick it in a Tupperware and don't forget your spoon (trust me—this can be very frustrating). The oatmeal puffs up when baked and it becomes almost like a fruity pudding. I tend to pack this with whatever berries are in season or in the supermarket.

## SERVES 6

1½ cups unsweetened almond milk

2 free-range eggs

2 tablespoons honey

1 teaspoon vanilla extract

¼ teaspoon almond extract

¼ teaspoon coarse sea salt

½ teaspoon gluten-free baking powder

1 teaspoon ground cinnamon

a pinch of nutmeg

2 cups fresh or frozen mixed berries (blueberries, raspberries, strawberries)

1 cup rolled oats

¼ cup flaked almonds

Preheat the oven to 350°F.

Grease an 8-inch baking dish. Mix the almond milk, eggs, honey, and vanilla extract together in a bowl. Add the salt, baking powder, and cinnamon and mix together.

Place half the berries on the bottom of the baking dish, cover with the oats then pour over the milk and egg mixture. Place the remaining berries on top, then sprinkle over the flaked almonds.

Bake for 40 minutes. Serve with a drizzle of honey.

## TIP

*Blueberries, raspberries, or strawberries all work well here—as does a mixture of all three. If using frozen berries, allow them to thaw before using.*

# BLACKBERRY BIRCHER MUESLI À LA SPRÜNGLI

This is based on the amazing Bircher Muesli made at the Sprüngli Café in Zurich, Switzerland. It's simply the best in the world. I have taken out the cream, but you could always add some in to taste, to make this dish even more luxurious. There is something so delicious about soaked oats with the crisp apple, the pops of fruitiness from the blueberries, and the sweetness of the banana. I tend to like this dish quite sweet, but if you want, you can always reduce the quantity of apple juice and, in its place, simply increase the unsweetened almond milk.

## SERVES 4

1½ rolled oats

1 teaspoon linseeds

1 teaspoon chia seeds

a pinch of ground cinnamon

a handful (½ cup) of blackberries (you can use raspberries too)

⅓ cup chopped almonds

1½ cups fresh pressed apple juice (not concentrate)

½ cup unsweetened almond milk

½ cup plain yogurt

1 apple, grated

½ banana, mashed

⅓ cup chopped pistachio nuts (I also love sugared hazelnuts, if you can find them)

Mix the oats, seeds, blackberries, and almonds with the apple juice, almond milk, and yogurt and leave to refrigerate overnight.

In the morning, add the apple and banana and mix in.

Serve with the chopped pistachio (or sugared hazelnuts) on top.

# MY BIGGEST INFUENCE: MY NANA

In my family, the old adage about things skipping a generation definitely applies to cooking. My nana was a wonderful cook and a glamorous hostess, always throwing parties. And it was she who taught me the basics, such as never letting your guests' drinks go dry and always keeping the food coming. My mom was not a natural in the kitchen. Her skills (and her sister's) were better suited to ordering off menus in restaurants (sorry, Mom). However, in me, my nana found a willing student.

Luckily, growing up in New York, I had plenty of cuisines to choose from. Nana always made us try out new tastes from all over the world—and from a very early age. Steaming bowls of Vietnamese pho with lemongrass and noodles, Chino-Cubano (a delicious Chinese–Cuban fusion cuisine which, as far as I know, only exists in Cuba, New York, and Miami), soy garlic and sesame shredded beef in our local Korean deli, and Israeli *mafrum* (think meatballs, but so much more juicy and delicious) from our local kosher eatery—everything was on our doorstep and my taste buds were attuned to spices, flavors, and ingredients well beyond my years.

Although Nana was American, she was born to Scottish parents who emigrated to New York with their young daughters in the 1920s. Her parents hailed from Glasgow ("Which was why they left," Nana always said!), and there was always an element of Scottishness to her personality, her cooking, and even her accent after a few glasses of wine. New Year's was always the best for that—after all the Champagne and some celebratory whisky, her accent would be in full force for *Auld Lang Syne*.

On the surface, my nana wasn't necessarily what you would picture when you think of the stereotypical kindly, soft-cheeked grandmother baking cookies for her grandchildren. She weighed scarcely 90 lbs, always had her hair done, and generally preferred a glass of Chardonnay and a cigarette in the evenings to baking cookies. But appearances can be deceiving, and she was a great cook and the most amazing grandmother.

My grandfather worked in the oil/energy industry and before retiring to Washington, DC, he and Nana had moved over 30 times, lived overseas for years (mostly in London), and had travelled the world with four children in tow. Nana had the best stories, always told nonchalantly, and nothing ever really fazed her.

She never forgot what it was like to be young, and she treated her teenage grandchildren as individuals, not children. She even encouraged our little rebellions, in her own way. I'll never forget one Christmas morning at her house: while we were all sitting around opening presents and having coffee, Nana suddenly looked over at the table next to her, picked up a heavy bronze lion's-paw ashtray she had got in Africa, and handed it to my 15-year-old brother saying, "Merry Christmas." She knew that my brother smoked (and that my dad hated it), but she also knew he was going to do it regardless, so he might as well have a cool ashtray!

My uncle also has a teenage memento from Nana. When he was at secondary school in London, he was dared by some friends to steal the wooden sign from outside their favorite pub. Having accomplished this, he found that the sign was too big to get into his tiny car. His solution was to call his mother. Nana, who was very understanding of the importance of teenage pranks, went to pick him and the wooden sign up and acted as his getaway driver!

For what Nana taught me about entertaining, see page 101, and for her apple pie recipe, see page 146.

# MY EVERYDAY PROBIOTIC SMOOTHIE

I know kale smoothies are all the rage, and I enjoy them myself from time to time, but I feel the focus on super-green juices and smoothies has made people forget how delicious fruit smoothies can be.

This is my favorite smoothie. It has a delicious, creamy texture from the banana and coconut yogurt and it's packed with super-healthy antioxidants and probiotics, all of which makes it the best way to kick-start feeling great every day. It is also my morning beauty elixir and makes such a difference to my skin. My skin has always been a barometer of my inner health—if something is off internally, it immediately sets my skin off—so as long as I am treating my body well from the inside, my skin will glow. There is lots of research showing the link between gut health, the immune system, and general mental and physical wellbeing, so I take probiotics every day—I use Beauty Chef Glow Inner Beauty prebiotic and probiotic powder. Prebiotics are a plant fiber that occurs naturally in onions, bananas, Jerusalem artichoke, chicory root, and beans. Prebiotics nourish the bacteria already in our gut—they are like food for the probiotics. Studies have shown that they can help anxiety, depression, and stress. Inulin, a prebiotic supplement, is being considered increasingly important for our gut health.

## SERVES 1

- 1 ripe banana, peeled and sliced
- 1 cup fresh or frozen blueberries
- ¾ cup coconut yogurt
- ½ cup unsweetened almond milk
- 1 to 2 frozen acai pellets
- 2 tablespoons runny honey
- 1 to 2 teaspoons prebiotic and probiotic powder

Combine all the ingredients in a blender and purée until smooth. Pour into a large glass and serve.

## INGREDIENT NOTE

*I use acai a lot in my smoothies—and it's great that you can get these frozen now in most supermarkets—along with blueberries, my other go-to smoothie fruit. Like goji berries, acai berries are considered a superfood. They are from the Amazon and have a great purple color. They are packed with antioxidants, amino acids, fiber, vitamins, and minerals—and are great for the health of your heart.*

# ICED RASPBERRY DANISH

Is there anything more delicious than a Danish? The crumbly flakes of the puff pastry, the fruity tang of the raspberry jam and the sweet pop of the icing? It's a one-way ticket to the perfect lazy weekend morning. If you have some frozen puff already pre-made then simply defrost and use a sheet of that, but for the quickest and easiest solution, store-bought is totally fine—I use GeeFree in the US.

## MAKES 6

1 cup ground almonds

⅓ cup superfine sugar, plus extra for sprinkling

2 tablespoons unsalted butter (room temperature)

1½ teaspoons cornstarch

2 medium free-range eggs

1 teaspoon almond extract (or Amaretto)

1 sheet gluten-free puff pastry (store-bought, or see page 183)

6 tablespoons good-quality raspberry jam

¼ cup sliced almonds, toasted

### FOR THE GLAZE

½ cup confectioner's sugar

1 tablespoon milk

Preheat the oven to 350°F.

In a food processor, mix the ground almonds, sugar, butter, cornstarch, one of the eggs, and almond extract into a paste and chill in the refrigerator while you prepare the rest of the ingredients.

Roll out the puff pastry sheet into a large square, big enough to allow you to cut six 4¾-by-4¾-inch squares.

Line a large baking sheet with parchment paper and transfer the squares to the baking sheet.

Beat the other eff and brush it around the edge of the squares. Add a tablespoon of the almond paste to the middle of each square, top with a tablespoon of raspberry jam, and add a sprinkle of flaked almonds.

Fold over the four corners into the middle and pinch together to form a small "hat." Brush with more egg and sprinkle a little extra superfine sugar over each pastry. Bake for 15 to 18 minutes, or until golden. Remove from the oven and place on a rack to cool.

Meanwhile, make the glaze by mixing the confectioner's sugar and milk until you have a smooth icing. When the pastries are cool, drizzle the glaze over each one and leave to harden. (If you are too impatient and it's too hot, the glaze will simply melt.)

# TOASTED ALMOND PANCAKES

## WITH FRESH BERRIES

While my brother always begged for French Toast, pancakes were my favorite breakfast treat. I used to have the whole collection of Disney character cutters! But now that I can't rely on traditional batter, creating a gluten-free version was very important to me. The almond flour and almond extract give these pancakes a gentle, nutty flavor, and the other gluten-free flours create a soft, fluffy result. The coconut oil is an amazing addition too—it gives a subtle sweetness and blends so well with the almond flavor. I love to serve these with fresh plums, but you can use any fresh fruits you like. The perfect start to a weekend morning.

## MAKES 15 PANCAKES

1¾ cups sorghum flour

1 cup almond flour

¼ cup potato starch (not flour) or tapioca

1½ teaspoons gluten-free baking powder

½ teaspoon fine sea salt

¾ teaspoon xanthan gum

1 cup unsweetened almond milk

1 cup water

2 medium free-range eggs, beaten

4 tablespoons coconut oil, melted, plus extra for frying

1 tablespoon honey

1 teaspoon vanilla extract

1 teaspoon almond extract (optional)

### TO SERVE

fresh plums/seasonal fruits, sliced almonds, maple syrup/honey, to serve

---

In a bowl, mix the dry ingredients and make a well in the center.

Gradually add in the wet ingredients and whisk to form a smooth batter.

Add a little coconut oil to a frying pan over a medium–high heat. Drop small ladlefuls of batter into the hot fat and cook until browned and bubbles begin to form on the surface, then flip with a spatula and cook for a further 1 to 2 minutes on the other side. Repeat until all the batter has been used up. Leave to cool on paper towels to mop up any excess oil.

Serve with fresh plums or seasonal fruits and berries with a handful of flaked almonds and drizzled with honey or maple syrup for an extra pop of sweetness.

## INGREDIENT NOTE

*Gluten free means taking out the gluten— sounds simple but when you take out the gluten—i.e. the elasticity—you have to replace it with something so that your dough stretches and binds so you don't just have crumbs. Xanthan gum is a great addition to gluten-free baking; don't add too much otherwise it will make your dough too heavy and glue-like.*

# GLORIOUSLY GLUTEN-FREE WAFFLES

Whether you want to go traditional and cover your waffle with fruit and syrup, go hipster and add these to my fabulous Buttermilk Fried Chicken (see page 115), or just add some crispy slices of bacon and a dash of maple syrup… the humble waffle is no longer hidden away in the bad-boy diner! Pile this gluten-free version high morning, noon, and night for total foodie satisfaction. You'll need a waffle iron.

## MAKES 6 STANDARD-SIZED WAFFLES

¼ cup sweet rice flour/ glutinous rice flour

¼ cup almond flour/ground almonds

½ cup brown rice flour

½ cup oat flour

½ cup tapioca starch

½ cup potato starch

1 tablespoon gluten-free baking powder

1 teaspoon sea salt

a pinch of ground cinnamon

1 cup buttermilk (or mix dairy or unsweetened almond milk with 1 tablespoon lemon juice)

4 tablespoons butter, melted

3 large free-range eggs

2 tablespoons honey

vegetable oil, to spray

Combine the dry ingredients in a bowl and then combine the wet ingredients in a separate bowl.

Make a well in the dry ingredients and whisk in the wet ingredients to make a batter. Allow the batter to sit at room temperature for 30 minutes before making the waffles—the baking powder will begin to react and the mixture will take on a "yeasty" appearance.

Spray some vegetable oil onto a waffle iron and use according to the manufacturer's instructions.

Place single waffles (do not stack or they will go soggy) onto a wire rack in a warm oven while you make the rest. Serve warm with your choice of toppings.

# LEEK AND ASPARAGUS QUICHE

This dish always reminds me of big family holiday brunches. When I first made it for my friends in the UK, they thought I was making them lunch in the morning and wondered what on earth this crazy American was doing to them. These days, I am pleased to say that the art of the New York brunch has become more common in Britain. The idea of serving asparagus and leeks for breakfast no longer raises quite as many eyebrows as it once did. But whether you have this for brunch or for lunch, it's delicious either way.

## SERVES 8

### FOR THE PASTRY
½ cup sweet rice flour/
  glutinous rice flour
¼ cup corn flour
¼ cup millet flour
¼ cup oat flour
¼ teaspoon sea salt
½ teaspoon xanthan gum
6 tablespoons cold unsalted
  butter, cut into pieces
3 tablespoons iced water

### FOR THE FILLING
2 leeks, chopped
3 scallions, chopped
olive oil, for frying
¼ cup oat flour
¼ cup sweet rice flour
4 large free-range eggs
1¼ cups whole milk
2 tablespoons chopped
  chives
3 ounces strong cheese (half
  Gruyère and half goat
  cheese would be perfect)
a pinch of nutmeg
8 ounces asparagus spears

Preheat the oven to 350°F.

**To make the pastry**, combine the dry ingredients in a large bowl. Add the butter and rub in until you have a sandy texture. Add in the iced water slowly and mix by hand until the dough begins to come together into a ball.

Flatten the dough into a 6-inch round, cover in plastic wrap and chill in the refrigerator for 30 minutes.

Roll out the dough on a gluten-free floured surface and gently lift into a 9-inch tart pan. Trim the edges, then place a disc of parchment paper on top and fill with baking beans. Bake blind for 10 minutes, remove the beans, and cook for a further 10 minutes. Remove from the oven and set aside.

**To make the filling**, sauté the leeks and scallions in olive oil over a medium heat for 10 minutes, until soft but not coloring. Set aside.

Place the flours in a bowl and make a well in center. Whisk the eggs and milk together and gradually whisk into the flours to make a smooth mixture.

Add the leeks and onions, chives, and cheese to the egg and flour mix (leaving the goat's cheese in clumps). Add the nutmeg.

Place the tart pan on a baking sheet and pour the mixture into the pastry shell. Arrange the asparagus in a circle on top, radiating from the center. Bake for 40 to 50 minutes, or until set and golden brown. Serve with a dressed arugula and radicchio salad, if liked.

# SWEET POTATO HASH

## WITH EGGS

This is great served with avocado. I sometimes add some hot sauce as well to give it a fiery kick to wake me up in the morning. I have used fresh thyme and oregano to flavor, but you could use half a bunch of fresh cilantro instead, which will also give it a lovely green herby taste.

### SERVES 2

2 tablespoons olive oil

1 onion, chopped

1 red bell pepper, chopped

½ green bell pepper, chopped

1 large sweet potato, diced into ½-inch pieces

1 garlic clove, thinly sliced

1 teaspoon chopped thyme

1 teaspoon chopped oregano

2 free-range eggs

sea salt and freshly ground black pepper

Heat the oil in a large, heavy-based frying pan and add the onions and peppers. Sauté over a medium heat for 5 minutes, then add the diced sweet potato. Cook, covered, for 10 minutes, shaking the pan occasionally.

Uncover and add the garlic and herbs and continue to cook until all the vegetables are tender and starting to color. Season with salt and pepper

Make two wells and crack an egg into each. Cook until the eggs are set, about 3 to 5 minutes, and serve.

## TIP

*You can cook the sweet potato ahead of time, if desired. Simply reheat before adding the eggs.*

# CHEESE AND HERB FRITTATA

The humble frittata is such a great staple for quick lunches or brunches—a classic dish that you can easily adapt to suit your whim. Traditional frittatas use flour, so I have removed that, and it works just fine with the eggs and baking powder. I love the combination of the earthy spinach, salty feta, and smoky cumin seeds.

## SERVES 4

2 tablespoons olive oil

1 small red onion, finely chopped

1½ cups baby spinach

10 free-range eggs

½ teaspoon coarse sea salt

½ teaspoon freshly ground black pepper

2 tablespoons chopped basil

2 tablespoons chopped mint

2 tablespoons chopped flat-leaf parsley

¾ teaspoon gluten-free baking powder

¼ teaspoon cumin seeds

½ cup feta cheese, crumbled

½ cup Parmesan, grated

Preheat the oven to 350°F.

Heat the oil in an oven-proof 10-inch deep frying pan over a medium–low heat. Add the onion and sauté for 5 to 7 minutes, or until soft. Add the baby spinach and cook, stirring, until wilted. Drain off any excess liquid.

Meanwhile, whisk the eggs, salt, pepper, and chopped herbs together. Add the baking powder and cumin seeds. Pour the egg mixture over the spinach and onion and top with the feta and Parmesan.

Return the frying pan to the heat for 2 to 3 minutes, to set the base, and then transfer to the oven. Bake for about 15 to 20 minutes, or until it is browned and puffed. It will be rounded and firm in the middle and a knife inserted in the center should come out clean. Serve hot.

# FILLING ZUCCHINI BREAD MUFFINS

The zucchini in these muffins makes them oh-so moist. They can be eaten pretty much any time of the day, but are especially perfect for an indulgent weekend brunch treat. Store them in an airtight container and they will last for a few days.

## MAKES 9

⅔ cup ground almonds
½ cup quinoa flakes
½ cup sorghum flour
¼ cup tapioca starch
2 teaspoons gluten-free baking powder
¾ teaspoon xanthan gum
¾ teaspoon sea salt
½ teaspoon ground cinnamon
½ cup maple syrup
¼ cup coconut oil, melted
2 free-range eggs
1 teaspoon vanilla extract
1 zucchini, grated

Preheat the oven to 350°F. Line 9 cups in a muffin pan with muffin wrappers or parchment paper.

Mix the dry ingredients together in a bowl. Whisk the syrup, coconut oil, eggs and vanilla extract in a separate bowl and then slowly add to the dry ingredients and mix in.

Squeeze any excess water from the zucchini and add to the mixture. Mix to combine, then spoon the mixture to fill the muffin cups three-quarters full.

Bake for 20 to 25 minutes until golden brown and firm to the touch.

These can be stored for up to 3 days in an airtight container.

## TIP

*It's a good idea to remove as much liquid from the zucchini as possible. Once grated, really squeeze the zucchini and drain off any liquid.*

# VEGETABLE STOCK

At the heart of all good cooking is a great stock. And at the heart of my stocks are time and care. Take time on these to give them depth of flavor. You don't need to buy fresh vegetables especially for this— you can use up older ones—although the older the veggies are, the less flavor you will get, so you may need to add more herbs. I put the stock into ice-cube trays and freeze them, so I can pop out a cube as and when I need it.

## MAKES 2 QUARTS

2 onions, peeled and quartered

10 celery sticks, roughly chopped

2 large carrots, roughly chopped

1 tablespoon oil

2 to 3 garlic cloves, roughly chopped

1 teaspoon sea salt

1 teaspoon black peppercorns

sprig of bay leaves

sprig of rosemary

Place the onions, celery, and carrots, with the oil in a large, heavy-based saucepan and cook over a low heat until the onions are softened. Cover with 3 quarts of cold water and add the garlic, salt, peppercorns, bay leaf, and rosemary.

Cover the saucepan and bring to the boil. Reduce the heat and simmer very gently for 1½ hours. Use a large spoon to skim off any scum that rises to the surface during cooking. Cool and skim again. Strain the stock through a sieve, pressing down the vegetable mush to release any further juices.

Refrigerate (for up to 3 days) or freeze (for up to 2 to 3 months).

# CLASSIC CHICKEN STOCK

Making a good stock was one of the first lessons I learned at culinary school, and I will never forget heaving huge pans full of bones into the industrial size pot we used. But the gorgeous, dark golden stock that resulted was truly amazing. Once you have had an authentic, slow-cooked stock you will never want to go back to that pale imitation that is store-bought stock.

## MAKES 2 QUARTS

2 raw chicken carcasses (available from most good butchers)

2 celery sticks, roughly chopped

2 carrots, roughly chopped (for a clearer stock, use leeks instead of carrots)

1 onion, peeled and quartered

1 head of garlic, halved, skin on

1 teaspoon black peppercorns

1 bunch of parsley (use stems only and save leaves for another recipe)

2 bay leaves

sprig of thyme

Place the carcasses, celery, carrots, onion, garlic, and peppercorns in a heavy-based saucepan and cover with 4 quarts of water. Tie the herbs into a bouquet garni with twine and place in the pan. Leave uncovered and bring to the boil. Simmer over a low heat for 4½–5 hours.

Cool and skim off the fat. Strain the stock through a sieve.

Refrigerate (for up to 3 days) or freeze (for up to 2 to 3 months).

# IT'S ALL G-G-GRAVY! MY BASIC GRAVY

When I first went gluten free, I thought it would be pretty obvious what I would have to give up—bread for sure, pasta, cakes, and cookies. It wasn't until I started really reading labels and paying attention to everything I was eating that I realized how many random foods have hidden gluten in them. Like Worcestershire sauce—surprise!—soy, and some chocolate. And gravy.

While a roux made with flour is certainly the classic base for gravy, there are plenty of other ways to thicken a sauce. The simplest is through reduction, but the addition of a cornstarch and water mixture can work too. This is called a slurry, and it's the go-to remedy for fixing even the most refined French sauces when they are on the watery side. Homemade gravy is a hundred times better than anything store-bought, and while some traditionalists insist on putting things like gizzards and giblets in their gravy (and if you're into that, be my guest), I personally have no need for giblets in my life—so I keep my gravy as simple as possible with a good, strong savory stock as its backbone. The starting point to any good gravy is always a pan of roasted meat and vegetables from the oven or a frying pan full of juices, if you have cooked the meat on the stovetop.

## MAKES 2 CUPS; SERVES 6 TO 8

roasting pan with meat and vegetables (see intro)
2 cups chicken or vegetable stock (see opposite)
1½ tablespoons cornstarch
sea salt and freshly ground pepper

### VARIATIONS

*For a delicious red wine gravy (perfect for roast beef or chicken), use 1 cup red wine and 1 cup stock.*

*To make a tasty cider gravy to go with roast pork, use 1 cup cider and 1 cup stock.*

*To turn this gravy into a rich pepper sauce (the ideal companion ro a steak) make the gravy as above and then stir in 2 teaspoons drained jarred pink peppercorns, 2 teaspoons brandy, and ⅓ cup heavy cream and simmer for 5 minutes.*

Remove the roasted meat (and vegetables) from the roasting pan or the meat from the frying pan. Pour off most of the fat, leaving behind the juices. Place the roasting pan/frying pan over a medium-low heat and gradually add the stock, stirring constantly to loosen any browned bits that are stuck to the bottom of the pan.

Once you've added the stock, transfer about 1 cup of the stock mixture to a medium bowl. Whisk in cornstarch until you have a smooth slurry. Return the slurry mixture to the roasting pan and whisk over a medium-low heat, stirring well, until thickened and smooth. Simmer gently for 5 to 10 minutes, adding a little more stock, if necessary, to reach the desired consistency.

Season with salt and freshly ground black pepper to taste. Serve with roast beef, lamb, chicken, or pork, or grilled sausages.

# WARMING CHICKEN GINGER AND RICE SOUP

No one likes to get a cold, especially when they're about to cater a charity dinner for some of the most important women in New York. I remember that day vividly: I woke up feeling terrible with a raw throat and hacking cough, but one of the girls on my team told me to chew a piece of raw ginger—and you know what? It worked. At least, enough to enable me to do the job. Ever since then, I always reach for the ginger before I ever start taking any medication. As well as helping with colds, ginger is also great for your digestion and it's an anti-inflammatory. Here, it's combined with the benefits of lemongrass, which is an antioxidant and helps keep aches and fevers at bay, giving you a soup to heal body and soul.

## SERVES 4

### FOR THE STOCK
2 lemongrass stalks, smashed
thumb-sized piece of fresh ginger, peeled and sliced
1 head of garlic, halved
3 shallots, peeled
8 whole black peppercorns
2 cups Thai basil
2 cups cilantro
2 cups parsley

### FOR THE SOUP
2 carrots, peeled and sliced
thumb-sized piece of ginger, peeled and finely grated
1 garlic glove, finely grated
1 to 2 tablespoons olive oil
½ cup basmati rice
3 skinless chicken breasts, seasoned
1 teaspoon sesame oil
cilantro, to garnish
sea salt and freshly ground black pepper

To make the stock, place all the ingredients in a large saucepan with 2 quarts water. Bring to the boil, then cover and simmer for 40 minutes and strain with a sieve.

In a separate saucepan, being the soup by sautéing the carrots, ginger, and garlic gently in the oil for 1 to 2 minutes, being careful not to burn the garlic. Add the rice and stir to coat in the oil.

Add the chicken breasts and then start to add the stock (6 cups at this stage). You will need a 2:1 ratio of stock to chicken and rice.

Cook over a gentle heat, uncovered, for 15 to 20 minutes or until everything is cooked. Remove from the heat.

Remove the poached chicken breasts from the pan and shred with a fork. Return the shredded chicken to the pan, season, and add another ladle or two of stock if you think it needs more liquid.

Add the sesame oil and cilantro to serve. Soul nourishment, guaranteed.

# SPANISH AJO BLANCO SOUP

This is the perfect light lunch or starter. Traditionally, this soup uses stale bread, which I have removed entirely. But I find that with the almond milk added to the water, it is still as creamy as the original. The trick with this dish is to use great olive oil and to make sure to serve your soup super cold. Who needs gazpacho when you have Ajo Blanco?

## SERVES 4

8 ounces blanched almonds, lightly toasted

6 tablespoons ice-cold water

¾ cup unsweetened almond milk

3 garlic cloves, roughly chopped

½ cucumber (about 7 ounces), peeled and roughly chopped

¾ cup plus 2 tablespoons extra virgin olive oil, plus a little extra to garnish

2 tablespoons sherry vinegar

8 seedless grapes, halved

sea salt and white pepper

Place the majority of the lightly toasted almonds into a blender or food processor (saving a few to serve). Add a dash of the water and blend for 30 seconds. Slowly add the rest of the water and the almond milk. Add the garlic, cucumber, olive oil, and vinegar. Blend until very smooth and then strain.

Add salt and pepper to taste, then chill in the refrigerator for at least 2 hours.

Chop the reserved almonds, and arrange on top of the soup with the grape halves and finish with a final drizzle of extra virgin oil.

## TIP

*To toast almonds, preheat the oven to 350°F. Spread the nuts in a single layer on a baking sheet and bake for 5 to 10 minutes, shaking occassionally. Remove as they turn golden brown.*

# LAMB AND GRAIN SOUP

My nana used to make this dish on Easter Monday as a good way to use up the lamb leftovers from Easter Sunday lunch. However, you don't need to wait until Easter to make this—it's equally great any time of the year.

I tend to serve this as a broth, but if you want a thicker soup consistency, you can always add a teaspoon of cornstarch (pre-mixed with water and with all the lumps removed) and stir in to thicken.

## SERVES 6

2 x lamb shanks (about 1lb 12 ounces) or 12 ounces cooked, shredded lamb

2 tablespoons vegetable oil

2 carrots (about 7 ounces)

1 onion

2 garlic cloves

1 celery stick

2 quarts Classic Chicken Stock (see page 38)

1 cup Job's tears (Chinese barley)

leaves from a few sprigs rosemary, chopped

leaves from a few sprigs thyme, chopped

sea salt and freshly ground black pepper

Season the lamb shanks, then brown them in 1 tablespoon of the oil in a non-stick frying pan (if you are using fresh meat).

Heat the remaining vegetable oil in a large, heavy-based saucepan and fry the carrots, onion, garlic, and celery. Add the browned (or pre-cooked) lamb to the sautéed vegetables. Then add the chicken stock. You want to keep the ratio of 2:1 stock to lamb and grain. Then add the barley and lastly the chopped herbs. Bring to the boil and cover and simmer over a low heat for 2 hours. Stir occasionally to ensure there is enough liquid and so nothing gets stuck on the bottom of the pan.

After 2 hours, remove the lamb shanks but keep the liquid boiling to reduce further. Take the meat off the bone and shred and return to the soup. Reduce the heat and cook for a further 5 minutes and then serve.

## INGREDIENT NOTE

*Job's tears, also known as Chinese barley, can be found at your local Chinese or Japanese supermarket, or at well-stocked natural foods stores. If you need an alternative, you can use oat groats, which are easier to find. Don't substitute for pearl barley, as this contains gluten.*

# ITALIAN MINESTRONE PASTA SOUP

This recipe calls for gluten-free dried pasta. Believe me, I have tried them all and each brand seems to work well in some dishes, but not others, so I do end up with quite a few different jars of pasta in my pantry. For this recipe, the best dried pasta is the tiny tube-shaped ditalini shells by Le Veneziane. You can buy this brand at many food retailers and via the internet.

## SERVES 4 TO 6

1 large (or 2 medium) zucchini, diced (about 9 ounces)

2 scallions, chopped

1 large carrot, diced (about 4 ounces)

6½ ounces green beans, diced

2 tablespoons olive oil

1 garlic clove, minced

1 unpeeled potato, diced (about 7 ounces)

3 tablespoons basil pesto

3½ cups chicken (or vegetable) stock (shop-bought or see page 38)

½ (14 ounce) can chickpeas

1 (14 ounce) can mixed beans/cannellini beans

1 cup ditalini pasta

a handful of basil, shredded, to serve

½ cup Parmesan, grated, to serve

sea salt and freshly ground black pepper

In a large, heavy-based saucepan, sauté the zucchini, scallions, carrot, and green beans in the olive oil over a low-medium heat for 5 to 10 minutes.

Add the garlic and potato and cook for a further 5 minutes. Keep stirring, so the garlic doesn't stick to the pan. Add the pesto and stock and bring to the boil. Add the chickpeas and beans and simmer, uncovered, for 10 minutes. Add the pasta and simmer for a further 10 to 12 minutes.

Season with salt and pepper and serve with the fresh basil and grated Parmesan.

# FORBIDDEN RICE SALAD

## WITH SESAME AND KALE

This recipe is inspired by a dish at one of my favorite gluten-free restaurants in New York—Siggy's Good Food. Tucked away on possibly the quietest block in NoHo, Siggy's has an amazing, unpretentious menu of organic, locally sourced comfort food and a relaxed atmosphere that feels like something of a haven. While they have my favorite gluten-free burgers in the city, the dish I find myself craving and ordering the most is their raw slaw—a huge plate of shaved kale, cabbage, and carrots, coated in a perfectly tangy lemon dressing with crunchy sesame seeds. This is my version and I've added one of my favorite grains—forbidden rice. This black heirloom rice was once eaten exclusively by Chinese emperors and is renowned for its health benefits.

I find this recipe is a perfect complete meal in itself, but it is also absolutely amazing served with seared fish or chicken and is one of my go-to sides when cooking larger dinners for friends.

## SERVES 8 FOR LUNCH (OR 12 AS A SIDE SALAD)

1 cup forbidden rice (or black rice)

7 ounces cavolo nero

14 ounces red or green cabbage

14 ounces carrots, grated

2 avocados

juice of ½ a lime

### FOR THE DRESSING

5 tablespoons fresh lime juice (about 3 to 4 limes)

1 tablespoon toasted sesame oil

2 tablespoons tamari

½ cup olive oil

¼ cup toasted sesame seeds

2 garlic cloves, minced

½ jalapeño pepper, ribs removed, minced

Place the rice and 1½ cups water in a medium-sized saucepan and bring to the boil. Cover with a well-fitting lid, turning the heat down to low and simmer for 35 to 40 minutes, until tender, stirring occasionally. Check towards the end of cooking that the rice isn't sticking to the pan. If it is, add a little more water. Once it's cooked pour the rice into a sieve, pour over boiling water to remove any excess starch, then spread out on a plate to steam dry and cool completely.

While the rice is cooking, cut the tough stalks from the cavelo nero and discard. Finely shred the leaves and put in a very large mixing bowl. Very finely shred the cabbage, using a mandolin, if you have one, then add to the mixing bowl along with the grated carrot.

In a separate bowl, mix together the dressing ingredients.

Add the cooled rice to the shredded vegetables, pour over the dressing and mix everything together.

Halve, stone, and peel the avocado, cut it into thin slices and squeeze half a lime over it to stop it discoloring.

Pile the slaw onto 1 or 2 large platters, then scatter the avocado slices on the top, ready for guests to help themselves.

# QUINOA, MANGO AND BLACK BEAN SALAD

This is one of my all-time favorite summer recipes due to its light, fresh flavors and also the particular feeling of summer that it evokes for me, whatever the time of year. The tender sweetness of the mango contrasts perfectly with the slight crunch of the quinoa and the saltiness of the black beans, while the hint of lime juice in the background heightens all the flavors. What a joy!

## SERVES 4

½ cup quinoa

3 to 4 corn cobs

olive oil

1 to 2 tablespoons olive oil

1 (14 ounce) can black beans, drained

3 ripe mangoes, peeled and cut into chunks

1 small red onion, finely chopped

sea salt and freshly ground black pepper

### FOR THE DRESSING

2 to 3 garlic cloves, minced to a paste

¾ teaspoon ground cumin

1 small–medium jalapeño, ribs removed, minced

½ cup fresh lime juice

½ cup extra virgin olive oil

1 teaspoon sea salt, to taste

½ teaspoon freshly ground black pepper, to taste

### TO FINISH

a small handful of cilantro, chopped

2 ripe avocados, chopped

Cook the quinoa according to the package instructions, drain off any excess water, and set aside to cool.

Cut the corn kernels off the cobs (to cut the corn, hold the cob near the top and, using a sharp knife, cut downward with a gentle sawing motion.) Sauté in olive oil and salt and pepper over a medium heat for 4 minutes. Transfer the cooked corn kernels to a large bowl.

Add the black beans, mangoes, and red onion to the bowl and stir in the cooled quinoa.

To make the dressing, mix all the ingredients in a small jar, pour into the bowl, and gently coat the salad. Add the chopped avocado last and season with salt and pepper, to taste.

# ZESTY BEET AND POMEGRANATE SALAD

Earthy and zesty in the same dish. The citrus of the orange perfectly offsets the deep purple density of the beets, and those oh-so sweet pops of pomegranate give this salad depth of flavor, as well as texture. Yet it's so super quick and easy to make.

## SERVES 2

1 pound beets
1 cup pomegranate seeds
1 small red onion, thinly sliced
1 tablespoon fresh orange juice
1 tablespoon grated orange zest
juice of ½ a lemon
¼ cup extra virgin olive oil
½ cup cilantro, roughly chopped

Preheat the oven to 400°F. Roast the beets in an ovenproof dish for around 30 to 45 minutes, depending on size, until tender. When cooled, peel, cut into chunks and transfer to a bowl.

Add the pomegranate seeds and red onion to the beets and mix.

In a separate small bowl, mix the orange juice and zest, lemon juice, and extra virgin olive oil until it forms a dressing. (I find shaking everything together in an old jam or jelly jar with a tight-fitting lid works well for dressings.)

Cover the beet with the dressing. Serve with the fresh cilantro.

# TABBOULEH QUINOA SALAD

## WITH CRISPY CHICKPEAS

I have started using Lebanese spices, such as sumac, more and more in my cooking. They add a great depth of flavor with often tangy notes, which lift dishes and give them a little bit of something new—and our taste buds love a new sensation! Sumac is quite citrusy and tangy, so you don't need to go crazy with the lemon juice. Give it a try, I think you will love it. I like to use tricolor quinoa for this dish as it retains a better bite, especially when cooled.

## SERVES 2 (OR 4 AS A SIDE DISH)

1 cup quinoa

2 cups vegetable stock (see page 38)

1½ cups can cooked chickpeas, drained

½ tablespoon olive oil

½ teaspoon cumin seeds

½ teaspoon freshly ground black pepper

¼ cup mint leaves, chopped

¼ cup parsley leaves, chopped

a handful of cilantro

1 cup cherry tomatoes, quartered

½ large cucumber, peeled, seeded, and diced

1 teaspoon lemon juice

1 to 2 tablespoons good-quality extra virgin olive oil

½ teaspoon sumac

pinch of sea salt

Cook the quinoa in the vegetable stock, according to the package instructions. Drain and leave to cool, then fluff up with a fork.

Meanwhile, in a bowl, coat the chickpeas with the olive oil, cumin seeds, and black pepper and fry over a medium–high heat for about 10 minutes, until golden and crispy. Set aside.

Mix the cooked quinoa with the herbs, tomatoes, cucumber, lemon juice, olive oil, sumac, and salt in a large bowl.

Add the crispy chickpeas to the salad and serve.

## INGREDIENT NOTE

*Used extensively all over the Middle East, sumac is a lemony spice that can be used on grilled meats and fish and also with homemade hummus. It's a deep red color, made from berries and comes in a coarse powder. It is often used instead of lemon juice as it's milder and less tart.*

# DELICIOUS ZUCCHINI FRITTERS

These are fantastic hot, but they work equally well the next day, cold from the refrigerator as a lunchtime snack. I usually serve them with a raw slaw (mix half a sliced red or green cabbage, 1 to 2 grated carrots, and 1 to 2 apples with ½ teaspoon cumin seeds, the juice of half a lemon, and 1 tablespoon Greek yogurt) or a simple green salad.

## MAKES 10 TO 12

3 cups grated zucchini
¾ cup gluten-free all-purpose flour
½ cup Parmesan, grated
½ teaspoon gluten-free baking powder
2 large free-range eggs
¼ cup mint, chopped
¼ cup parsley, chopped
2 scallions, finely chopped
zest of 1 lemon
2 tablespoons vegetable oil
sea salt, for sprinkling

Place the zucchini in a sieve and sprinkle with salt. Leave for 30 minutes, then squeeze out all the liquid between several sheets of paper towels, which will also remove any excess salt. Transfer to a bowl.

In another bowl, make the batter by mixing the flour, Parmesan, baking powder, and eggs.

Mix the zucchini with the herbs, scallions, and lemon zest.

Add the zucchini mix to the batter. If the mixture is too wet, add a little more flour.

In a frying pan, heat the oil over a medium heat. Form the zucchini mixture into patties using 2 tablespoons of the mixture and place in the frying pan. Cook for 2 to 3 minutes or until golden brown, flip, and repeat to cook the other side.

Remove the patties from the pan and transfer to paper towels to remove any excess oil. Keep cooking until all the mixture has been used.

Serve hot or cold with your choice of slaw or salad.

# ASIAN SUMMER ROLLS

## WITH PEANUT AND CHILE DIPPING SAUCE

### MAKES 8

2 ounces rice vermicelli noodles

8 rice paper wrappers

16 large shrimp, cooked and halved

2 sprigs of mint leaves, roughly chopped

4 sprigs of cilantro, roughly chopped

1 small carrot, peeled and grated

1 Little Gem lettuce heart, shredded

1 tablespoon peanuts, roughly chopped

### FOR THE DIPPING SAUCE

1 teaspoon sugar

2 tablespoons lime juice

2 tablespoons crunchy peanut butter

1 tablespoon fish sauce

1 garlic clove, crushed

1 red chile, finely chopped

So easy to make, so fresh and so healthy. I always keep rice paper wrappers in my cupboard, so I can whip this dish up in an instant for a quick meal. These little rolls are so addictive that I usually end up making a couple of batches at a time. I also find this is one of the dishes that kids love to help you make—the process of making the little parcels always entertains them, especially if they break!

Cook the rice vermicelli noodles according to the packet instructions, but make sure they are al dente. Rinse in cold water and drain thoroughly, so they don't get soggy. Set aside.

Fill a bowl with cold water and submerge the rice paper wrappers for 10 to 20 seconds until almost soft, but not so soft they break. (Most packages usually have their own instructions.)

Lay the rice paper on a board and place 2 shrimp with a pinch of the herbs in the centre of each. Add a pinch of carrot and a small clump of rice vermicelli. Finish with some shredded lettuce and a sprinkling of chopped peanuts, making sure you leave enough of an edge for rolling and take care not to overfill or they will break.

Bring the bottom edge of the rice paper over the filling, then fold the sides in like an envelope and roll up tightly.

To make the sauce, mix the sugar and lime juice until the sugar has dissolved. Add the remaining ingredients and mix. Serve in a little bowl with your summer rolls for dipping.

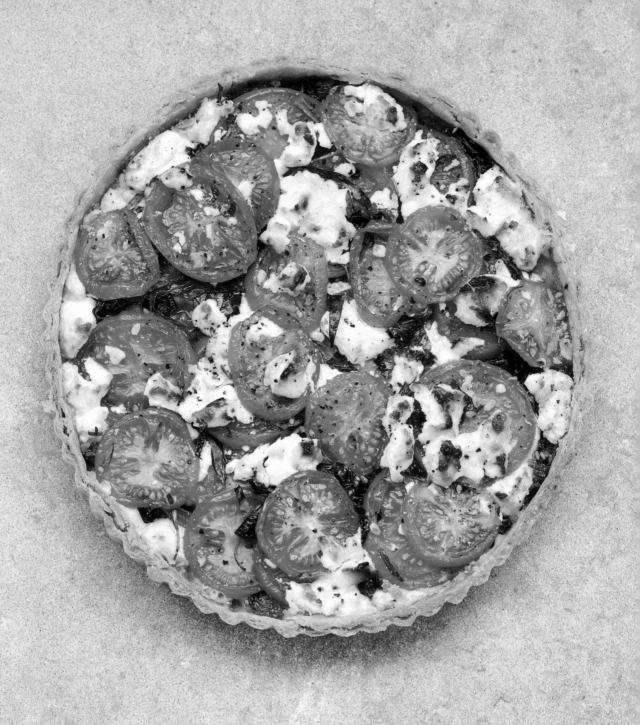

# TOMATO AND BUCKWHEAT TART

As I mentioned in my introduction, despite its name, buckwheat is a good friend to the gluten-free cook as it's made from a fruit, not wheat—confusing, huh? Its earthy, nutty flavor and darker color makes it the perfect backdrop to the rich tomatoes, tangy goat cheese and sweet caramelized shallots. Pretty dreamy.

## SERVES 6 TO 8

### FOR THE BUCKWHEAT PASTRY

½ cup sweet rice flour/ glutinous rice flour

½ cup buckwheat flour

¼ cup cornstarch

½ teaspoon xanthan gum

¼ teaspoon sea salt

6 tablespoons unsalted butter, cut into pieces and chilled

4 tablespoons ice-cold water

### FOR THE FILLING

4 ounces shallots, chopped

1 tablespoon butter

pinch of granulated or coconut sugar

several sprigs of thyme, chopped

4 ounces goat cheese, crumbled

4 large beefsteak tomatoes, thinly sliced, horizontally

3 tablespoons extra virgin olive oil

several springs basil, leaves picked and chopped

1 sprig tarragon, leaves picked and chopped

½ tablespoon honey

To make the pastry, combine the dry ingredients in a large bowl. Add the butter and rub in until it resembles breadcrumbs. Add the iced water slowly and mix by hand, until the mixture comes together to form a smooth ball. Roll out the dough to fit a 9-inch loose-bottomed tart pan. Lift the dough using a rolling pin and gently place into the pan. Press firmly into the pan and trim off any excess pastry. Chill in the refrigerator for 20 minutes before baking.

Preheat the oven to 400°F.

To make the filling, caramelize the shallots in a saucepan with the butter and pinch of sugar over a medium-high heat for 8 minutes and set aside to cool slightly.

Remove the tart shell from the refrigerator. Spread the caramelized shallots and thyme on the bottom of the shell and sprinkle with some of the goat's cheese.

Place a layer of tomatoes on top and add a drizzle of extra virgin olive oil, and some basil and tarragon. Repeat the layers to fill the tart, finishing with a layer of goat's cheese and a drizzle of honey on top.

Bake for 25 to 30 minutes, until golden and the pastry is cooked and beginning to pull away from the sides of the pan. Cool before serving.

# SPAGHETTI ALLA NERANO

This is a version of a dish that I first had at the restaurant Quattro Passi in Nerano, Italy. It became something of an addiction and it was wonderful to find they had opened a restaurant in London. However, back in New York I still had to satisfy my craving for this dish, and so I worked out my own version. For this I use Ancient Harvest Quinoa gluten-free spaghetti.

## SERVES 4

1¼ pounds small–medium zucchini (yellow and/or green), cut crosswise into thin coins

2 garlic cloves, minced

2 tablespoons olive oil

14 ounces dried spaghetti

leaves from a few sprigs basil, leaves picked

2 teaspoons lemon juice

pinch of sea salt

½ teaspoon cracked black pepper

grated Pecorino cheese, to serve

Sauté the zucchini and garlic in olive oil over a low–medium heat for 10 to 12 minutes, until soft. Remove and dry on paper towels to remove excess oil.

Place the dried spaghetti in salted boiling water and cook until al dente according to packet instructions. Drain, reserving ¼ cup pasta water.

Place half the zucchini in a blender with the reserved pasta water, adding the basil, lemon juice, salt, and black pepper. Blitz to a purée.

Return the purée, remaining fried zucchini, and cooked spaghetti to the pan and heat over a medium heat for 2 to 3 minutes, until warmed through.

Serve with a generous grating of Pecorino cheese.

# MUJADARA

## WITH CARAMELIZED SHALLOTS

There is a reason why nearly every Middle Eastern country has a version of this dish—because it tastes so good! And it's so simple too: rice, lentils, and onions—that's pretty much it. But the combination creates something that will become one of your go-to comfort dishes. It works as a standalone dish, but equally can be served as a side dish as it just goes with everything. I often use it alongside chicken.

### SERVES 8

2 tablespoons vegetable oil

1 teaspoon cumin seeds

½ teaspoon freshly ground black pepper

4 large onions, sliced

½ teaspoon ground cumin

1 cinnamon stick

2 cups Basmati rice

1⅓ cups can green or brown lentils, drained

4 cups chicken (or vegetable) stock (store-bought or see page 38)

zest and juice of 1 lemon

1 cup flaked almonds or pine nuts

sea salt and freshly ground black pepper

Add the vegetable oil to a heavy-based frying pan. Add the cumin seeds and black pepper and sauté for about 1 minute or until it smells aromatic. Add the onions and sosalt and cook until they turn golden brown and caramelize, stirring often, so they don't burn. This will take about 15 minutes. Using a slotted spoon or spatula, transfer half of the onions to a plate lined with kitchen paper and reserve for later.

Sprinkle in the cumin and then add the cinnamon stick. Sauté for about 1 minute. Add the rice and coat with the oil and spices. Add the lentils, stock, and a pinch of salt, bring to the boil, then turn to low and simmer, covered, for 30 minutes, until the rice is soft. (If there's still stock in the bottom, replace the lid and cook for a further 5 minutes.) Turn off the heat. Remove the lid and cover with a clean tea-towel to allow the rice to steam, undisturbed, for about 5 minutes.

Meanwhile, toast the almonds or pine nuts in a small skillet over a medium-low heat, shaking often, for about 5 minutes.

Check the rice for seasoning and fork through the lemon zest and juice. Serve garnished with the reserved caramelized onions and toasted almonds or pine nuts.

# SUPER GREEN FALAFEL

The origin of the word falafel means "little balls," and there is a reason that these little deep fried balls are so popular throughout the Middle East. I love to freshen up the density of the traditional falafel with herbs. I use fresh, but you can used dried herbs as well. I prefer to use dried chickpeas, which I soak in boiled water with baking soda. If you want to use canned chickpeas instead, use 2 x 14-oz. cans and add 2 tablespoons chickpea flour— this soaks up any extra moisture and avoids the falafel getting too wet.

## MAKES ABOUT 20

12 ounces dried chickpeas, rinsed

½ teaspoon baking soda

1 large red or yellow onion, finely sliced

3 garlic cloves, chopped

3 teaspoons coriander seeds, crushed

2 teaspoons sea salt

1 teaspoon ground cumin

½ teaspoon freshly ground black pepper

2 teaspoons gluten-free baking powder

4 tablespoons buckwheat flour or chickpea flour

1 to 2 tablespoons harissa paste

3 tablespoons chopped cilantro

3 tablespoons chopped flat-leaf parsley

vegetable oil, for frying

### FOR THE TAHINI SAUCE

1 small garlic clove, grated

2 tablespoons lemon juice

5 tablespoons ice-cold water

1 large roasted red pepper

1 teaspoon sea salt

¼ teaspoon superfine sugar

1½ teaspoons sweet paprika

½ cup tahini

Place the chickpeas and baking soda in a saucepan and add enough cold water to cover them by at least 2 inches. Bring to the boil over a high heat and boil for 2 minutes. Remove from the heat, cover with a lid and let soak for 1 hour. Drain.

For the tahini sauce, combine the garlic, lemon juice, and water in a food-processor and purée until the mixture is nice and frothy. Add the roasted red pepper (buy these ready roasted or grill over a hot heat for a few minutes until the skin burns, remove and when slightly cooler remove the scorched skin), salt, sugar, and sweet paprika; purée until smooth and then gradually add in the tahini to create a creamy sauce. Set aside.

For the falafels, combine the onion and garlic in a food processor and pulse until finely ground. Add the chickpeas and coriander seeds and pulse until the chickpeas are just broken down. Add the salt, cumin, pepper, baking powder, and flour and pulse until the mixture is finely chopped. (Make sure not to purée into hummus!) If the mixture is a little too wet, simply drain off any excess liquid.

Transfer half the falafel mixture to a separate mixing bowl. Add the harissa to the bowl (to taste), working it in until it evenly colors the mixture. Add the cilantro and parsley to the remaining falafel mixture in the food processor and pulse until the herbs are finely chopped.

Roll both mixtures into balls (about 1½ inches in diameter).

Heat a couple of inches of oil in a large frying pan over a medium heat. Add 6 to 8 falafel balls at a time to the hot oil (this can be a mixture of the green and red) and cook for about 1½ minutes or until they are golden brown and cooked through. Remove with a slotted spoon and transfer to paper towels to drain off any excess oil. Repeat until all the falafel balls are cooked. Serve warm or at room temperature, with the sauce for dipping.

# LINGUINE

## WITH SHRIMP, LEMON, AND PARMESAN

There are some pasta dishes in this book where I have gone for fresh options, but sometimes dried pasta is the perfect choice—and for everyday dishes like this, for an easy supper for four or more, I always use the dried gluten-free store-bought version. I find that Rummo is a brand that always works—it's Italian, so it should be good!

### SERVES 4

14 ounces gluten-free dried linguine

1 tablespoon butter

2 garlic cloves, grated

1 pound raw shrimp, peeled

juice of 2 lemons

½ teaspoon grated lemon zest

1 tablespoon chopped oregano

2 tablespoons chopped parsley, plus extra to serve

½ teaspoon sea salt

½ teaspoon freshly ground black pepper

1½ cups light cream

1 cup Parmesan, grated plus extra to serve

Boil the dried pasta in slightly salted and oiled water following the packet instructions until al dente, drain, and set aside. (With GF pasta always go al dente, otherwise the pasta goes too soft and gloppy.)

Melt the butter in a saucepan over a medium heat. Gently sauté the garlic for 1 to 2 minutes, or until softened.

Add the shrimp and cook until they start to become pink and opaque. Add the lemon juice and zest, oregano, parsley, salt, and pepper, and cook over a low heat for 2 to 3 minutes.

Add the cream and stir, until it starts to bubble. Add the Parmesan and continue to stir, until it's incorporated into the sauce. Remove from the heat, add the drained pasta to the sauce and toss to coat evenly.

Serve with extra Parmesan, parsley, and freshly ground black pepper to taste.

# FEEDING THE MANY

## FOR LARGER GROUPS AND SPECIAL OCCASIONS

I absolutely love entertaining. The most fun I have in the kitchen is when I'm cooking for large groups of friends and family. It's also how I learned to cook—in front of an audience. So this section is packed with ideas about how to pull off those gatherings for larger groups of people and have fun doing it!

When I started cooking, it was for my mom's bridge class. Each week, the hostess would try to outdo her friends with fresh-out-of-the-oven home-baked goods, salads, or cold cuts. My mom is a wonderful woman and a fabulous parent, but, as I have mentioned, cooking has never been her forte. But who was to know that she had a 12-year-old secret weapon, hidden away in the family kitchen. I would bake fluffy spinach and cheese muffins, thickly iced chocolate cupcakes, warm gooey cookies, all of which my mom would proudly present. Everyone loved the food at her bridge sessions. And that was my first taste of catering to a group. Now I have my own catering company, and as I prepare for another crazy Fashion Week event, I often think back to those formative years, learning to cook in quantity and for a highly critical audience.

These days, as much as I like going out to eat, I hate the hassle of having large tables in a restaurant—the food is never as good and there is always an argument over the bill. I would much rather have my friends over to my house and cook good food for them, with no bill! I know the idea of "entertaining" seems sort of old-fashioned these days, particularly in New York, where it is so common to eat out or order in nearly every night (and afternoon) of the week. But I truly feel that the art of entertaining is due for a comeback. I love the thought of the "pop" of the first cork, the smell of canapés baking in the oven, fresh flowers on the table, and lighting my candles just before the doorbell kicks into action.

You don't need to spend a huge amount of money on entertaining—if you choose a clever menu and make cocktails in pitchers, then the cost per head becomes manageable. The art is to be bountiful—that is really at the core of being a great host or hostess.

# GRILLED TANDOORI CHICKEN

## WITH COCONUT RAITA

One of my favorite things about growing up in New York was the exposure I got to so many different types of food at a very young age. One of my absolute favorites was tandoori chicken. So you can imagine how excited I was when I moved to London and got to explore just a fraction of its incredible Indian restaurants. Most of us don't have a tandoor oven at home, but I've found that tandoori chicken works incredibly well on the grill. And so my favorite childhood meal has now become my default dish for any summer barbecue. Traditional raita is a cucumber–yogurt sauce used to balance out the spices in the dish it accompanies. For this version, I have used coconut yogurt. In my opinion, it's by far the best non-dairy yogurt-thick and tangy with the subtle coconut, adding another layer of flavor to this amazing dish and making it just as refreshing, but dairy free as a bonus. It can be made a day in advance, with the flavors just melding more and tasting even better.

## SERVES 8 TO 10

### FOR THE CHICKEN

3 (3½-pound) chickens, each cut into 8 pieces, all kept on the bone (you can ask your butcher to do it)

14 ounces coconut yogurt

juice of 2 lemons (about 6 tablespoons)

1 jar (about 10 ounces) tandoori paste

4 garlic cloves, minced

thumb-sized knob of ginger, peeled and chopped

2 tablespoons garam masala

### FOR THE RAITA

14 ounces coconut yogurt

1 large cucumber, halved, seeded and diced

1 teaspoon ground cumin

leaves from a few sprigs of cilantro, roughly chopped

leaves from a few sprigs of mint, roughly chopped

pinch of sea salt

juice of 2 limes (about 4 tablespoons)

To prepare the chicken, remove the skin and make 2 to 3 slashes through to the bone. This will help to push the marinade flavors and the heat from the grill into the meat when cooking.

In a bowl, mix together the coconut yogurt, lemon juice, tandoori paste, garlic, ginger, and garam masala. Coat the chicken pieces in the mixture and marinate in the refrigerator for at least 2 to 4 hours.

Remove the chicken from the marinade and cook on a hot barbecue grill for about 25 minutes, turning occasionally. Alternatively, cook in 2 batches under a hot grill for about 25 minutes, making sure to keep the first batch warm, covered with foil in a roasting pan, in a low oven (225°F).

To make the raita, put all the ingredients in a bowl, mix together, and refrigerate until ready to use.

To serve, pile the chicken pieces onto a large platter and serve with a bowl of raita, ready for guests to help themselves.

# STICKY SESAME CHICKEN

## WITH TAMARI BROWN RICE AND SHIITAKE MUSHROOMS

This is such a great dish to make for a simple kitchen supper. It's really all about the sauce, which despite having quite a few ingredients, is quick and easy to make. I love Sriracha. It's a hot sauce, originally from Thailand, made from chiles, garlic, vinegar, sugar, and salt. In Thailand it's often a side for seafood, but I think it works brilliantly with chicken as well, and it gives this dish a really nice, hot kick.

## SERVES 4

### FOR THE CHICKEN

1 free-range egg

2 tablespoons cornstarch

1 pound free-range skinless chicken breast, cut into strips

1 tablespoon vegetable oil

1 cup broccolini

1 cup sugar snaps

sea salt and freshly ground black pepper

### FOR THE RICE

1 cup brown rice

½ tablespoon sunflower oil

1 garlic clove, minced

5 scallions, chopped

1 teaspoon red chile flakes

1 cup shiitake mushrooms, cut or torn into bite-sized pieces

### FOR THE SAUCE

2 tablespoons tamari

¾ inch piece fresh ginger, peeled and grated

1 garlic clove, grated

½ tablespoon sesame oil

1 tablespoon cornstarch

1½ tablespoons honey

1½ tablespoons rice wine vinegar

½ tablespoon Sriracha

### TO SERVE

1 tablespoon sesame seeds, toasted

2 to 3 scallions, sliced

Begin by cooking the chicken. Mix the egg with the cornstarch. Season with salt and pepper and toss the chicken strips in the mixture.

Add the vegetable oil to a hot wok and fry the chicken over a medium–high heat until golden brown, about 8 minutes. Set aside.

In a saucepan, cover the brown rice with salted water and bring to the boil. Simmer for 40 to 45 minutes or until the rice is cooked, then drain. Place the oil in a frying pan and fry the garlic, scallions, and red chile flakes over a medium heat. Add the shiitake mushrooms and cook until golden, adding a teaspoon of water if the pan becomes too dry. Add to the rice and mix.

To make the sauce, mix all the ingredients together with 1 teaspoon water in a bowl. Gently heat in a wok over a medium heat.

Meanwhile, place the green vegetables in a steamer over boiling water for 4 to 5 minutes, or until they are cooked, but still have some bite. Set aside.

Place the golden chicken in the wok and coat with the sauce. Serve with the rice, toasted sesame seeds and sliced scallions and the vegetables on the side.

# GRILLED BASIL CHICKEN

## WITH SAFFRON, CORN, AND BURNED ZUCCHINI

I have always loved Israeli food, and I am so excited that it has recently become one of the hot trends on the London restaurant scene. Palomar in the West End is a particular favorite of mine, and their Burned Zucchini Tzatziki is to die for. I wanted to create a dish that nods to the amazing flavors and cooking of Israel, and I love the way zucchini takes to being burned; it gives it so much more flavor and texture and is a great addition to this dish.

### SERVES 6

1 cup basil, roughly chopped

1 garlic clove, chopped

juice and zest of 1 lemon

2 tablespoons olive oil

6 skinless chicken breasts

3 to 4 lemons, halved, for grilling

2 large zucchini

½ cup butter

pinch of saffron

3 corn cobs

sea salt and freshly ground black pepper

Preheat the oven to 350°F.

Put the basil, garlic, lemon juice, and zest with some salt and pepper in a blender. Add the olive oil to loosen and blitz to a purée.

Cover the chicken with half the basil marinade and refrigerate for at least 2 hours. Reserve the other half for later.

Remove the chicken from the marinade, and place under a hot broiler with the lemon halves for 2 to 3 minutes per side. Transfer to an ovenproof dish and cook for 20 minutes.

Meanwhile, slice the zucchini horizontally into slices, ½-inch thick and season with salt and pepper. Brush with a little oil and fry on a hot griddle pan until almost burned.

Melt the butter in a saucepan over a low heat and add the saffron.

Halve each corn cob horizontally, using a sharp knife. Coat the corn in the melted butter and broil for 5 minutes on each side until cooked and slightly charred.

Keep the leftover butter mixture warm for serving over the corn.

When ready to serve, gently warm the rest of the basil marinade over a low heat and serve with the hot chicken, buttered corn cobs, and burned zucchini.

# DUCK CARNITAS

## WITH SPICED MANGO AND CORN TORTILLAS

### MAKES 12

4 duck legs, skin on

3 teaspoons sea salt

1 teaspoon black pepper

1 onion, quartered

2 dried chipotle chiles

1 head of garlic, halved

1 tablespoon whole black peppercorns

2 whole star anise

1 cup duck fat

### FOR THE SPICED MANGO

1 mango, peeled and diced

juice of 1 lime

2 tablespoons diced red onion

2 tablespoons chopped cilantro, plus extra to serve

½ yellow pepper, diced

1 tomato, diced

⅛ teaspoon chipotle powder

### TO SERVE

2 Little Gem lettuces

12 corn tortillas (see page 186)

lime juice, to taste

Made with masa harina flour, corn tortillas are naturally gluten free. You can make them fresh (see page 186) or buy them; either way, when they are combined with succulent duck and zesty mango salsa, it's total heaven in a tortilla. The duck is spiced with smoky chipotle chiles. These dried, smoked chiles date back to the Aztecs, and they are a little less harsh than standard dried chiles. This dish makes a delicious weekend lunch for four.

Rub the duck legs with the salt and pepper and refrigerate for at least 12 hours.

Preheat the oven to 325°F.

Place the duck legs, skin-side down, in an ovenproof frying pan set over a medium heat and cook for 12 to 15 minutes, until the fat from the skin renders out of the legs and they become golden and brown.

Add the onion, chipotle chiles, garlic, peppercorns, star anise, and duck fat. Cover the pan with foil and place in the oven for 2 hours.

To make the spiced mango, place all the ingredients in a bowl and mix. Leave to chill in the refrigerator for 30 minutes.

After the duck has cooked for 2 hours, remove the foil, increase the oven temperature to 400°F and cook for a further 20 minutes. Set aside for 10 minutes.

Once rested, remove the legs from the pan, discard the remaining fat and flavorings, and shred the slightly cooled duck meat.

To assemble, take a single lettuce leaf and place in the middle of a tortilla, then fill with duck and spiced mango. Repeat with the remaining lettuce and tortillas. Serve with extra cilantro and add lime juice, to taste.

# LAMB KEFTA

## WITH CRISPY ZA'ATAR POTATOES AND HERB SAUCE

I am all about Middle Eastern flavors at the moment, and za'atar is at the core of a lot of my favorite dishes. Traditionally, it's a mix of thyme, oregano, marjoram, roasted sesame seeds, sumac, and salt, and it is often used in baking, which is how I first came across it. Za'atar works so well with potatoes and complements the lamb kefta in this recipe beautifully. (Make sure to pick a brand that has no flour added—check the ingredients list.) I serve this dish with a herb sauce, just to give it a little lift.

### SERVES 4 TO 6

**FOR THE KEFTA**

1½ pounds minced lamb

1 small white onion, finely chopped

1 teaspoon turmeric

1 teaspoon ground cinnamon

1 teaspoon ground cumin

1 teaspoon cumin seeds

1 teaspoon sumac

1 teaspoon sea salt

½ cup cilantro, chopped

2 tablespoons pine nuts

2 tablespoons golden raisins, chopped

2 medium free-range eggs, beaten

olive oil, for frying

**FOR THE ZA'ATAR POTATOES**

1 pound new potatoes

1 tablespoon za'atar

1 tablespoon olive oil

**FOR THE HERB SAUCE**

2 cups cilantro

2 cups parsley

3 tablespoons lemon juice

½ cup extra virgin olive oil

¼ cup pine nuts

sea salt and freshly ground black pepper

Preheat the oven to 375°F.

First, prepare the potatoes: boil them in water until soft, then drain, and crush them with a fork—but do this gently, so they are still partially intact. Toss with the za'atar, olive oil, and some seasoning to coat. Place the spiced potatoes on a baking sheet lined with parchment and roast in the oven for 35 minutes, until crispy.

Meanwhile, prepare the kefta. Put all the ingredients, except the olive oil, in a large bowl and mix well with your hands. Shape into golf-ball-sized balls until all the mixture has been used.

Heat a large, heavy-based frying pan over a medium-high heat. Add the oil and fry the keftas, until browned on all sides and cooked through. Set aside and keep warm.

To make the sauce, place the herbs, lemon juice, oil, and pine nuts in a blender and blitz to a purée. Add an extra dash of oil if the sauce needs loosening and season, to taste.

Serve around 3 to 4 kefta per person with the potatoes and a green salad, drizzled with the herb sauce.

# VELVETY BEEF BOURGUIGNON

When the rain is pouring and the wind is roaring, this is the perfect winter dish. I serve it with one of my baguettes, hot from the oven (see page 174) or some creamy mashed potatoes (celeriac purée is a great side as well). It's a complete hug on a plate. I have added a tablespoon of brandy to my recipe for a real depth of flavor, but it's by no means essential.

## SERVES 6

1 tablespoon vegetable oil

1½ pounds boneless chuck beef, cut into 1-inch cubes

2 tablespoons cornstarch

5 ounces pancetta, diced (or bacon lardons)

¾ pound pearl onions, peeled

½ pound shiitake and button mushrooms, mixed and sliced

1 large carrot, quartered lengthwise and sliced

1 tablespoon brandy

bouquet garni (2 peeled garlic cloves, slightly crushed, 4 black peppercorns, 2 sprigs of thyme, 1 bay leaf, 1 sprig of parsley)

1 bottle (3 cups) red wine

fresh flat-leaf parsley, chopped, to serve

Preheat the oven to 300°F.

Heat half the oil in a heavy-based saucepan over a medium heat. Dust the beef pieces in cornstarch and fry for 3 to 4 minutes on each side, until browned. Do this in 3 batches and set aside.

Lower to a medium heat, add the remaining vegetable oil and fry the pancetta, pearl onions, mushrooms, and carrot for 5 minutes. Add the brandy and bouquet garni and cook for 2 to 3 minutes. Add the beef, 6 tablespoons of water, and the red wine and bring to the boil. Remove from the heat and transfer to a casserole dish. Cut a piece of baking parchment the size of the dish and place loosely on top.

Cook in the oven for 90 minutes and serve topped with parsley and your choice of side dishes.

## TIP

*This is a great dish to cook in advance. It can be chilled for up to 2 days before reheating, and it tastes even better when reheated.*

# SALMON WELLINGTON

This is a showstopper of a dish. There is something satisfying about making your own pastry from scratch, but if you don't have the time, then shop-bought is fine too. You can also use skinless salmon fillets and make individual parcels.

## SERVES 6

2 shallots, finely chopped
3 tablespoons butter
3 leeks, finely chopped
1 garlic clove, minced
¼ cup dry white wine
juice and zest of 1 lemon
2 pounds frozen spinach, thawed
½ cup watercress
⅓ cup heavy cream
½ cup chopped parsley
¼ cup chopped tarragon
¼ cup chopped dill
2 tablespoons chopped chives
1 side of salmon, skinless, at room temperature
1 block of homemade Puff Pastry (see page 183) or 2 sheets store-bought gluten-free puff pastry
2 free-range eggs, beaten
sea salt and freshly ground black pepper

Preheat the oven to 400°F.

In a heavy-based frying pan, sauté the shallots in the butter over a medium heat. Add the leeks and sauté to soften. Add the garlic and soften for a further minute.

Deglaze the pan with the white wine, lemon juice, and lemon zest. Add the spinach and wilt down. Add the watercress and wilt, then add the cream and stir over a low heat. Add the fresh herbs, then remove from the heat and leave to cool, discarding any excess liquid.

If you are using my Puff Pastry recipe, take the fully thawed puff pastry (if frozen) and halve the block. Return one half to the refrigerator. Roll out the half block onto a sheet of parchment paper until it is longer and wider than the salmon. It should be the thickness of a quarter. If you're using store-bought sheets, roll one out now.

Place the salmon, flat-side down, on the pastry. Make sure there is a border (about ½ inch) running around the whole salmon, so you can seal it. Season the salmon with salt and pepper then cover with the spinach and watercress mixture, coating the fish evenly.

Remove the second piece of puff pastry and roll it out bigger than the first piece, so that it will cover the salmon completely. Brush the edges of the bottom piece of pastry with beaten egg, then lay the other piece on top. Fold it over to make a parcel, entirely enclosing the salmon. Mould the pastry around the fish with your hands, then press the edges with a fork to seal, cutting off any excess pastry. (Use up any spare pastry pieces by making them into shapes to decorate the top of your Wellington. Use egg wash to attach them.)

Chill the pastry-wrapped salmon in the refrigerator to make sure that the pastry is nice and cold before cooking.

Make 4 to 5 scores across the top of the pastry parcel, to allow any steam to escape and brush all over with the beaten egg. Cook in the center of the oven for 25 minutes, until golden brown and crisp. (The time may vary, depending on the thickness of the salmon.) Serve.

# SICILIAN SWORDFISH

## WITH TOMATO AND OLIVE SAUCE

Also known as Swordfish Palermitana, this is one of the best ways I have found to cook this amazing fish and keep it moist. Those Sicilians know a thing or two about cooking and the mixture of the crispy breadcrumb coating with the pops of sweet and sour from the raisins, capers, and sun-dried tomatoes whisks me off to Palermo in an instant.

## SERVES 4

4 swordfish steaks (about 5 ounces each)

1 cup dried gluten-free Panko (Japanese style) breadcrumbs

½ tablespoon chopped sun-dried tomatoes

½ tablespoon chopped capers

1 garlic clove, finely chopped

2 tablespoons finely chopped flat-leaf parsley

3 tablespoons extra virgin olive oil

juice of 1 lemon

sea salt and freshly ground black pepper

### FOR THE TOMATO AND OLIVE SAUCE

3 ounces raisins

2 tablespoons olive oil

1 small onion

1 garlic clove, sliced

½ pound tomatoes, chopped

10 green olives, pitted and chopped

2 ounces pine nuts

¼ cup capers

pinch each of sea salt and freshly ground black pepper

Preheat the oven to 400°F.

To make the sauce, soak the raisins in water for around 30 minutes, then drain. Heat the olive oil in a frying pan over a medium heat and sauté the onion and garlic until soft. Add the plumped raisins, tomatoes, olives, pine nuts, and capers. Cover the pan and cook for 10 minutes.

To prepare the fish, remove any skin and season.

Place the dried breadcrumbs, sun-dried tomatoes, capers, garlic, some salt and pepper, and the parsley in a wide, shallow bowl and mix. In a separate bowl, mix the olive oil and lemon juice.

Coat one side of the swordfish steaks with the olive oil and lemon juice mixture and then coat in the breadcrumb mixture. Turn the fish and, again, coat in oil first, then breadcrumbs. Repeat until all the steaks are coated.

Line a baking sheet with parchment paper. Place the swordfish steaks on the sheet and bake for 10 minutes. Be careful not to overcook. The steaks should feel firm. On the inside the fish will have turned from translucent to cream/white. It should be just cooked through to the middle.

Crisp up the steaks by heating up a nonstick griddle pan on the stovetop, over a high heat, and cook each steak for about 4 minutes on each side until golden.

Serve the steaks with the sauce served to preference, either on top or on the side.

# TAMARI SALMON

## WITH COCONUT RICE

Soy is one of those annoying things that you have to avoid when going gluten-free, as it contains wheat. Luckily, we have tamari instead. Japanese in origin, it is a by-product of miso and has a slightly richer flavor, but it does the trick for me. I also tend to find tamari has a gentler flavor when you bake rather than pan fry with it. This recipe serves a good party of people, but you can easily reduce the amount of salmon for a smaller meal for a few friends.

### SERVES 10

3 tablespoons honey

3 tablespoons tamari

1 garlic clove, minced

juice of 2 lemons (about ⅓ cup)

2 tablespoons sesame oil, plus 2 tablespoons olive oil, mixed

2 whole salmon fillets (each about 1 pound 10 ounces), skin on

### TO SERVE

leaves from 1 bunch cilantro, chopped

1 lime, cut into wedges

sea salt and freshly ground black pepper

### FOR THE RICE

2 small white onions, finely chopped

1 tablespoon vegetable oil

1 pound 2 ounces basmati rice

1 (14 ounce) can coconut milk

Preheat the oven to 350°F.

Make up the marinade for the salmon. Place the honey, tamari, garlic, lemon juice, and olive and sesame oils in a bowl. Place the salmon fillets in the marinade and chill in the refrigerator for at least 2 hours.

Remove the fillets from the marinade and place in a baking dish, skin-side up. Season with salt and pepper, then spoon half of the marinade over each fillet.

Line 2 baking dishes (1 for each 1½-pound side) with parchment paper and bake the fillets for 25 to 30 minutes. Slice each 1½-pound piece into 5 pieces after cooking.

To make the rice, soften the onions in vegetable oil in a saucepan over a medium heat for 10 minutes. Make sure you don't caramelize them. Add the rice and coat in the oil.

Add the coconut milk and 1¾ cups water. Simmer over a medium heat and cover. Cook for 15 minutes, until fluffy and soft.

Place the salmon on the rice, spooning over any cooking juices. Sprinkle with the cilantro, a dash of tamari, and some wedges of lime to serve.

## INGREDIENT NOTE

*Tamari is a great alternative to soy. Richer in flavor and color, it is also made from soybeans but Japanese tamari has no wheat in it. It's also less harsh on the palette than soy.*

# FRIED SOLE

## WITH PARSNIP CHIPS AND TARTAR SAUCE

I remember first encountering the British phenomenon of fish and chips as a child. We were sitting in a car, in the rain. As soon as we opened the hot paper packages, the windows of the car steamed up! The memory of my first taste of crispy batter encasing the freshest, flakiest cod, and the hot, fluffy chips, smothered in vinegar and salt is a very fond one that is as British to me as my nana's Sunday roasts. It's virtually impossible to find fish and chips that good outside of the UK—and I would never try to recreate the perfect fish supper (let's leave that to the chippie), but perhaps this version is a little healthier than the original?

## SERVES 6

8 parsnips, peeled and cut into thumb-sized chips

1 tablespoon olive oil

2 tablespoons chopped flat-leaf parsley

1 tablespoon chopped chives

⅓ cup polenta

¼ cup ground almonds

¼ cup gluten-free breadcrumbs

2 garlic cloves, minced

zest of 2 lemons

1 teaspoon celery salt

1 teaspoon freshly ground black pepper

2 free-range eggs

6 sole fillets (or any other flat fish such a flounder, around 4 to 5 ounces per fillet)

6 tablespoons vegetable oil

### FOR THE TARTAR SAUCE

¾ cup mayonnaise

3 tablespoons capers, drained

3 tablespoons gherkins, drained and chopped

1 small shallot, finely chopped

1 tablespoon lemon juice

2 tablespoons chopped parsley

1 tablespoon chopped chives

pinch each of sea salt and freshly ground black pepper

Preheat the oven to 400°F.

To make the tartar sauce, place all the ingredients in a food processor and blitz for 30 seconds. Chill in the refrigerator until ready to serve.

In a saucepan of boiling water, blanch the parsnips for 4 to 5 minutes. Remove from the water, drain, and coat them in the olive oil.

Transfer to a baking dish and cook in the oven for 20 to 25 minutes, until golden brown. Remove from the oven and lower the temperature to 250°F.

In a wide, shallow bowl, mix the herbs, polenta, almond flour, breadcrumbs, garlic, lemon zest, celery salt, and pepper.

In a separate wide, shallow bowl, beat the eggs.

Dip a fillet of fish in the egg, then coat in the polenta mixture, ensuring the whole fish is covered. Repeat again to coat all the fillets.

In a frying pan, start by heating half the vegetable oil over a medium-high heat. When the oil is hot, fry the fish for 3 minutes on each side, until the crumb is golden brown. You may have to fry in 2 to 3 batches, so make sure the oil is replenished and hot before each batch. Keep the cooked fish warm in the oven.

Serve the fish with the parsnip chips and tartar sauce.

# GOOEY CAULIFLOWER PARMIGIANA

One of my top restaurants is Senza Gluten in NYC. It's 100 per cent gluten free. If you are ever in town, you have to stop by—and always go with an empty stomach! This is my version of their amazing Parmigiana—it's one of my all-time favorites, so I hope I have done it justice. For breadcrumbs I tend to use Ian's.

## SERVES 4

### FOR THE TOMATO PURÉE

2 white onions, diced

2 tablespoons olive oil

1 garlic clove, finely chopped

2 (14 ounce) cans whole Italian tomatoes

½ teaspoon sea salt

½ teaspoon granulated sugar

¼ stick unsalted butter, cubed

### FOR THE PARMIGIANA

1 large cauliflower, divided into large florets

½ cup gluten-free plain flour

2 free-range eggs, beaten

¾ cup gluten-free breadcrumbs

1 to 2 tablespoons olive oil, plus extra for drizzling

1 cup Parmesan, grated

½ pound mozzarella, torn into chunks, leaving several pieces sliced, for topping

First make the tomato purée. In a heavy-based saucepan, over a medium heat, sauté the onions in the olive oil, until soft, then add the garlic and soften.

Add the tomatoes, bring to the boil, then simmer and reduce down. This will take about 45 to 60 minutes and the mixture will darken in color and reduce by about a quarter. Add the salt, sugar, and butter, then set aside to cool. Transfer to a food processor or Vitamix and blitz to a purée.

Next, make the Parmigiana. Preheat the oven to 350°F.

Place the cauliflower florets in boiling salted water and parboil for 5 minutes. Remove and plunge immediately into a bowl of iced water. Dry off the florets.

Coat the florets in the gluten-free flour. Then coat in the egg wash and, finally, roll in the breadcrumbs.

Pour a layer of tomato purée into the bottom of a large round casserole (about 9 inches wide x 3 inches deep), then sprinkle some Parmesan over the top. Cover with a layer of cauliflower and then scatter with torn pieces of mozzarella. Repeat. For the top layer, use the remaining tomato purée, then sprinkle the remaining Parmesan and finish with mozzarella. Drizzle with olive oil. Bake for 25 to 30 minutes, until golden and bubbling.

# ARANCINI DI RISO

## WITH TOMATO SAUCE

Originally, I would make arancini as intended by countless generations of prudent Sicilian cooks—in the traditional way of using up leftover risotto—but there was never enough to go round. So now I make the risotto from scratch, just so I can make the arancini. I serve them with a tomato sauce and a green side salad for a bigger lunch dish. They are also great for snacks or canapés and can be assembled in advance and kept covered in the refrigerator for up to 8 hours, until ready to fry.

### SERVES 6 TO 9 (MAKES 18 BALLS)

2 tablespoons olive oil

1 onion, finely chopped

2 cups uncooked carnaroli risotto rice

6 cups hot vegetable stock

2 cups fine dried gluten-free breadcrumbs

3 large free-range eggs

½ cup flat-leaf parsley, finely chopped

½ cup Parmesan, grated

4½ ounces mozzarella, divided into 18 pieces

canola or vegetable oil, for frying

sea salt and freshly ground black pepper

### FOR THE TOMATO SAUCE

2 small onions, finely chopped

3 tablespoons olive oil

2 garlic cloves, minced

2 tablespoons tomato pureé

2 (14 ounce) cans whole Italian tomatoes, chopped

pinch of sea salt

pinch of sugar

10 to 12 basil leaves, shredded

To make the risotto, heat the olive oil in a small saucepan, add the onion and cook for 10 minutes until soft. Stir in the rice and cook for 1 to 2 minutes, then add a ladleful of stock. Keep stirring, until most of the liquid has been absorbed by the rice, then add another ladleful. Continue gradually adding the stock and stirring for about 18 minutes, until the rice is mostly soft, but with a little bite in the center. Season to taste, then pour into a wide, shallow dish to cool quickly. Once cool, refrigerate until ready to assemble.

Now make the sauce. In a heavy-based saucepan, sauté the onion in 2 tablespoons of the olive oil over a low to medium heat until soft, then add the garlic and tomato pureé and cook for a further 3 minutes. Add the tomatoes, salt, and sugar, and cook over a low heat, partly covered, for 40 minutes. Add the basil and the remaining tablespoon of olive oil to loosen. Add salt and pepper to taste.

In a bowl, mix the cooked (and fully cooled) risotto rice, half the breadcrumbs, 1 of the eggs, the parsley, and Parmesan, plus salt and pepper to taste.

In a separate bowl, beat the remaining eggs and set aside. Place the remaining breadcrumbs in a wide, shallow bowl.

With slightly damp hands, mold a ball from the risotto mix, about the size of a tangerine (about 3 ounces). Make a hole in the middle of the ball with your finger and pop a small piece of mozzarella inside (be careful not to overfill), then close and re-form, ensuring the mozzarella is entirely enclosed in risotto. Continue until you have used all the risotto mixture and mozzarella pieces.

Fill a large saucepan with at least 3 to 4 inches vegetable oil and heat to 325°F. Use a thermometer to keep the temperature constant. Dip the balls in the beaten egg, then roll in the breadcrumbs, coating them entirely. Working in batches, with a slotted spoon, drop the balls into the hot oil and fry for 10 minutes, until golden brown. Remove from the oil and transfer to paper towels to soak up any excess oil. Eat within 24 hours.

# EGGPLANT GRATIN

We say eggplant; in the UK they say aubergine. In Asia it's brinjal. Whatever its name, this fabulous deep purple fruit is a favorite all over the world, due to its earthy, meaty flavor. If you are avoiding meat, it's a great substitute. Fry it, dip it, roll it, curry it—it's the most versatile of ingredients.

For this recipe, you can always add ground lamb to make it into a moussaka. Personally, I love the simple flavors of this meat-free version.

## SERVES 4 TO 6

### FOR THE TOMATO SAUCE
2 onions, chopped
2 tablespoons olive oil
2 (14 ounce) cans tomatoes
1 teaspoon dried basil
½ teaspoon celery salt
½ teaspoon freshly ground
     black pepper
¼ teaspoon ground nutmeg

### FOR THE GRATIN
2 large eggplants (about 11
     ounces each)
2 cups Parmesan, grated
1 cup basil leaves, shredded

Preheat the oven to 400°F.

To make the tomato sauce, sauté the onions in the olive oil for 10 to 15 minutes over a medium heat, until soft. Add the remaining ingredients and simmer gently for 45 to 50 minutes, until you have a lovely, thick sauce.

Meanwhile, prick the skins of the eggplants with a fork and roast whole, until soft. This will take about 30 minutes. Leave to cool and cut into slices ¼-inch thick. Drain off any excess water.

Pour half the tomato sauce into the bottom of a casserole dish, then sprinkle generously with a third of the Parmesan and half the shredded basil. Cover with half the sliced eggplant, then repeat with the sauce, Parmesan, basil, and eggplant. Sprinkle the remaining Parmesan on top.

Bake for 30 minutes until the gratin is bubbling and the top is golden brown all over.

Leave to sit for 10 minutes before serving (so you don't burn the roof of your mouth) and let the aroma fill your kitchen.

# GLUTEN-FREE PASTA

I love Italy and I love pasta. So it's quite lucky for me—and you—that some brands have got their gluten-free dried pastas to such a high standard in the last couple of years. In this book, I have given details of some of my favorite brands for different pasta shapes: Ancient Harvest, Le Veneziane, and Jovial are all great gluten-free brands and I recommend that you have them in your cupboard. But as good as they are, there is something about fresh pasta, especially gluten-free fresh pasta, that takes a dish to another level. Yes, it seems like a bit of a hassle, and it's not for every night, but I thoroughly recommend both the process—which is strangely therapeutic—and, most importantly, the eating, for when you really need a treat in the pasta department. You'll need a pasta machine.

## MAKES 4 SHEETS

¾ cup corn flour, plus more for rolling
¼ cup tapioca starch
¼ cup potato starch
¾ cup masa harina
scant ½ cup brown rice flour
1 teaspoon xanthan gum
1 teaspoon sea salt
4 large free-range eggs

Mix the flours, xanthum gum, and salt in a bowl. Make a well in the center, break in the eggs and mix to a dough. Knead until smooth and divide into 4 pieces.

Sprinkle a work surface with some cornstarch. Roll out each piece of dough, then transfer to a pasta machine.

Start on the first setting and work down the settings to medium. With gluten-free dough, do not try and work this down to the highest setting as it will start to fall apart.

When you have a flat sheet of pasta about the thickness of a dime, use a sharp knife and handcut into lengths, varying the thickness, depending on the dish.

Cooking time is 4 to 5 minutes.

## TIP

*Dust your work surface and rolling pin generously with corn flour to keep the dough from sticking.*

# FRESH GLUTEN-FREE TAGLIATELLE

## WITH PESTO, KALE, AND PINE NUTS

This is a twist on one of my all-time favorite pasta dishes: spaghetti with pesto. I'll always remember the first time I had classic Genovese pesto in Cinque Terre (a beautiful string of small towns which cling like seabirds' nests to the steep cliffs of the Italian Riviera). It had just the most incredible creamy texture with the fresh, bright flavor of the basil.

In my version, the addition of the kale lends a dark green heartiness. So as well as being delicious, this meal makes the pasta seem like a virtuous health food. After all, with all that kale how could it not be?

### SERVES 4 TO 6

4 rolled sheets fresh pasta (see page 89) cut into tagliatelle lengths

7 ounces kale, ribs removed

3 to 4 tablespoons olive oil

2 garlic cloves, peeled

1 teaspoon sea salt

juice of ½ lemon

### FOR THE PESTO

3½ ounces kale, ribs removed

⅓ cup pine nuts, toasted

juice of ½ lemon

3 to 4 garlic cloves, crushed

3 cups basil

½ cup olive oil

### TO SERVE

½ cup Parmesan, finely grated

¼ cup pine nuts, toasted

olive oil, for drizzling

Start with the pesto. Roughly chop and blanch the 3½ ounces kale in a pot of boiling, salted water for 30 seconds. Transfer immediately to a bowl of iced water, then drain and wring dry with a towel.

In a food processor, combine the garlic, Parmesan, pine nuts, salt, and lemon juice and pulse to a paste. Add the blanched kale and basil and pulse again. With the food processor running, slowly stream in the olive oil, until smooth.

Drop the fresh tagliatelle into a large saucepan of boiling salted water. As this is gluten free and fresh, cook it, as always, al dente. Remove from the heat after 3 to 4 minutes, drain (reserving some of the water) and set aside.

Cut the 7 ounces kale lengthways into long thin strips, to mirror the appearance of the tagliatelle.

Heat a large frying pan over a medium–high heat. Once hot, add 3 to 4 tablespoons olive oil and sauté the kale strips. Once the kale starts to wilt, add the garlic cloves and sea salt and sauté until kale is softened and the garlic begins to brown (but not burn). Remove from the heat and squeeze lemon juice on top of the mixture.

Combine the tagliatelle with the pesto and enough of the pasta water (about 6 tablespoons) to form a creamy sauce, adding more pesto as needed. Finally, add in the kale strips mixture and toss together with tongs.

To finish, add the toasted pine nuts, some freshly grated Parmesan and a drizzle of olive oil.

# VENETIAN PASTA PARCELS

## WITH BROWN BUTTER, SAGE, AND POPPY SEEDS

These little parcels of bright red beet are completely adorable—and a great way to entice children into eating beets. There is just something so satisfying when you combine butter and sage—I could almost eat it on its own—and the poppy seeds give this dish an extra level of texture.

### SERVES 6

6 sheets fresh pasta (see page 89)

#### FOR THE FILLING

5½ cups raw beet
2 tablespoons olive oil
1 cup ricotta cheese
¾ cup Parmesan, finely grated, plus extra to serve
pinch of sea salt and freshly ground black pepper
pinch of nutmeg

#### FOR THE SAUCE

1 stick butter
½ cup sage leaves
1 tablespoon poppy seeds

Preheat the oven to 375°F.

Wash and quarter the beets. Place on a baking sheet, drizzle with olive oil, sprinkle with a pinch of salt, and roast in the oven until soft (around 30 to 40 minutes).

Once the beets have cooled, remove the skins and blitz in a food processor with the ricotta and Parmesan. Add a pinch of sea salt, black pepper, and nutmeg and mix. Set aside.

Take 2 fresh pasta sheets and roll onto a piece of parchment paper. Cut 3-inch circles with a cookie cutter or a small glass into each sheet. (You can re-roll trimmed pasta to make extra circles.) Repeat with the remaining pasta sheets.

Take 2 circles of pasta for each parcel. In the middle of 1 circle, place a generous teaspoon of filling. With a finger, wet the edge of both circles and lay one on top of the other. Using your finger, seal the edges firmly, so there are no air pockets. Chill the parcels in the refrigerator for 30 minutes.

Meanwhile, make the brown butter sauce by melting the butter in a frying pan over a medium heat. Add the sage leaves and cook until they turn crispy, then add the poppy seeds and cook for a further 30 seconds. Remove from the heat and set aside.

Add a pinch of salt to a large saucepan of water on a rolling boil, and slowly drop the parcels into the water. Cook for 3 minutes or until they rise to the surface. Remove the parcels from the boiling water with a slotted spoon and place onto plates.

Quickly reheat the brown butter sauce and then drizzle over the pasta. Serve with grated fresh Parmesan.

# SICHUAN PEPPER MAITAKE MUSHROOMS
## WITH SPINACH

This is the perfect side dish, but I am also very partial to eating it on its own for a light lunch—often with a bowl of sticky rice as an accompaniment. The pepper in this dish gives it a little kick, but I find this is happily offset by the earthy warmth of the mushrooms and the spinach. Really quick and simple and also very good for you.

### SERVES 2

1 tablespoon olive oil

1 shallot, finely chopped

1 cup fresh maitake mushrooms (if you can't get maitake, shiitake mushrooms will make a good substitute)

1 garlic clove, chopped

¼ teaspoon Sichuan peppercorns, lightly crushed

2 cups baby spinach

juice of 1 lime

Heat the oil in a wok over a medium heat. Add the shallot and sauté for 2 minutes. Then add the mushrooms, garlic, and Sichuan peppercorns and fry for a further 3 minutes. Add the spinach and wilt down, then add the lime juice, to taste.

### INGREDIENT NOTE

*Sichuan pepper is used in Chinese and Indian cooking, as well as Tibetan and Nepalese. If you ever use five spice powder, you will have used it before! It is not as hot and punchy as chile or black pepper; it's more lemony. It's great thrown in the wok with oil, ginger, and garlic, and works with meat like chicken, duck, and pork, and noodles.*

# WARM ARTICHOKES

## WITH MELTED MOZZARELLA

I first had this amazing lunch dish at Da Armando al Pantheon in Rome. Italy is all about fresh flavors and wonderful textures, and this dish ticks all the boxes for me. The best thing about it is that it looks like you have gone to a lot of effort, yet it's so easy to pull off (just don't tell your guests).

### SERVES 4

4 artichoke hearts (frozen or fresh)

1 garlic clove, thinly sliced

2 tablespoons olive oil, plus extra for drizzling

2 lemons, 1 juiced and 1 cut into wedges, to serve

1 teaspoon red pepper or chile flakes

¼ cups parsley, chopped

9 ounces mozzarella, torn

sea salt and freshly ground black pepper

In a frying pan, sauté the artichoke hearts and garlic in the olive oil, over a medium heat for 5 minutes, turning occasionally until golden. Transfer to a saucepan, cover with water, and add the lemon juice. Cover and simmer for 12 to 15 minutes. Remove the hearts from the heat and drain.

Sprinkle the hearts with the red pepper or chile flakes and chopped parsley and season well. Drizzle with olive oil and serve with torn fresh mozzarella and lemon wedges.

# STIR-FRIED ASIAN VEGETABLES

## WITH SESAME AND CHILE

This dish is just so flexible as well as being super quick. It goes with pretty much any fish or meat—and it's the perfect way to spice up any leftover vegetables as well. I probably make this at least once a week—once you have all the ingredients in your pantry then you will find it an absolute go-to recipe.

### SERVES 4

2 teaspoons peanut oil

3 garlic cloves, sliced

1 red chile, thinly sliced

1¼ pounds mixed hearty greens, including bok choy, broccoli raab, or baby spinach

1 tablespoon tamari

2 teaspoons toasted sesame seeds

1 teaspoon sesame oil

Heat the peanut oil in a wok. Remove the wok from the heat and add the sliced garlic and chile. Let them cook in the hot oil for 1 minute, making sure the garlic does not burn.

Return the wok to the heat, add the vegetables and stir-fry for 3 to 4 minutes. Add 1 tablespoon water to add steam to help wilt the vegetables. Remove from heat, add the tamari, sesame seeds, and sesame oil to coat the vegetables. Serve hot.

# PURPLE POTATO SALAD

Like pretty much everyone on the planet, I love potatoes. Mashed, baked, roasted, or fried, they are deliciously addictive in almost any form imaginable. The only potato dish that never appealed to me was the ubiquitous potato salad, served at the summer barbecues of my childhood. Cold, bland, and generally overly gloppy with mayonnaise, it did not do the noble potato justice.

It wasn't until I was a teenager and was lucky enough to travel to Paris, where I had my first French potato salad, that I understood the true, delicious potential of this dish. After experimenting back at home, I discovered that while it is key to toss the potatoes in the vinaigrette while still warm, so that they fully take on all the flavors, the salad itself is just as delicious—if not more so—served cold, once the potatoes have had a chance to absorb all the delicious dressing even more.

I wanted to give this dish a bit more of a modern twist with the fresh color of the purple potatoes. A bit of jalapeño gives it some heat and the scallions, red onion, and fresh lime juice give a little pop to a classic recipe. All in all, this is a far cry from the bland, monochrome potato salad of my childhood.

## SERVES 6

- 2 pounds purple potatoes, peeled and cut into medium chunks
- ½ cup scallions, chopped (about 7 in all)
- 1 jalapeño, seeded and diced
- 1 tablespoon Dijon mustard
- 3 tablespoons tarragon leaves, finely chopped
- ¼ cup olive oil
- 1 small red onion, diced
- 1 garlic clove, mashed into a paste
- 2 teaspoons sea salt
- 1 tablespoon fresh lime juice
- 2 tablespoons Champagne vinegar

Cook the potatoes a saucepan of simmering salted water for 8 to 10 minutes, until tender, then drain.

While the potatoes are cooking, mix the rest of the ingredients together in a large bowl.

Turn the warm potatoes into the dressing and mix together well.

Serve warm or cold.

# SHALLOT AND HERB LABNEH

## WITH CRISPY MUSHROOMS AND JERUSALEM ARTICHOKE CHIPS

You might have started seeing labneh popping up on menus and on TV cooking shows recently. A creamy, tangy Middle Eastern yogurt (sometimes called "yogurt cheese"), this is a great side or dip. It does take a little bit of preparation and some forward planning, but it's really simple to make and such a wonderful alternative to either cream cheese or plain Greek yogurt. I have mixed it here with shallot and herbs as the perfect accompaniment for some mushrooms and Jerusalem artichokes (also known as sunchokes, and not to be confused with regular artichoke hearts).

### SERVES 4 TO 6

12 ounces Greek yogurt

¼ teaspoon lemon juice

3 shallots, peeled and finely sliced

8 tablespoons good-quality olive oil

3 medium-sized Jerusalem artichokes, peeled

canola or vegetable oil, for frying

2 pounds mixed mushrooms (oyster, button and shiitake), thickly sliced

1 small garlic clove

juice of ½ lemon

1 tablespoon za'atar

1 teaspoon chopped chives

1 teaspoon chopped thyme

1 tablespoon chopped tarragon

1 tablespoon chopped basil

sea salt and freshly ground black pepper

In a bowl, combine the yogurt, lemon juice, and pinch of salt.

Over a separate bowl, line a colander with 2 layers of muslin. Spoon the yogurt mix into the muslin. Transfer the bowl with the colander to the refrigerator for 12 to 24 hours. The longer you strain, the thicker the labneh. Remove from refrigerator and discard the liquid in the bowl.

In a frying pan, sauté the shallots in 2 tablespoons of the olive oil, until caramelized and just crispy brown. Drain on paper towels and set aside to cool.

To make the chips, slice the artichokes with a mandolin and dry off any excess moisture on paper towels. Fill a wok or saucepan with about 2 inches of vegetable oil and heat to 325°F (keep the temperature constant—cooking at a higher temperature can make the artichokes taste bitter). Fry the artichoke slices in batches for 30 to 60 seconds, until lightly golden, then remove with a slotted spoon. Dry off any excess oil on paper towels and sprinkle with salt.

Meanwhile, coat the mushrooms in 3 tablespoons of the olive oil and season to taste. Preheat the oven to 450°F. Line a baking sheet with parchment paper and bake the mushrooms on for 25 minutes.

To make the shallot and herb labneh, blitz the garlic, lemon juice, 2 tablespoons of the olive oil, za'atar, and herbs in a small food processor or blender to form a herb oil. Stir two-thirds of the herb oil into the labneh. If the mixture is too thick, simply loosen with extra lemon juice and olive oil. Check the seasoning, drizzle with the remaining herb mixture and last tablespoon of olive oil and sprinkle with the crispy shallots just before serving. Remove the cooked mushrooms from the oven and place on a serving plate. Sprinkle with the crispy Jerusalem artichokes and serve alongside the labneh.

# FABULOUS GLUTEN-FREE STUFFING CUPS

These wonderful little cups are made from cubes of gluten-free bread and cooked in muffin pans—giving 12 individual servings that really add a little bit of unexpected fun to a roast dinner. I like to freshen up my stuffing, so I have used cranberries, pecans, orange zest, and herbs as the flavorings, but these can be substituted for other dried fruit or nuts, as desired. Perfect with Thanksgiving turkey, roast chicken, or even your gluten-free Christmas dinner.

## SERVES 4 TO 6, MAKES 12

12 slices white gluten-free bread (about 14 ounces)

1 tablespoon olive oil

8 tablespoons butter

2 slices cured bacon, chopped (optional)

1 onion, sliced

2 celery sticks, diced

½ cup cranberries

½ cup pecans, chopped

2 teaspoons chopped sage

1 teaspoon chopped rosemary

1 teaspoon thyme leaves

finely grated zest of 1 orange

3 tablespoons potato flour

2 large free-range eggs, beaten

sea salt and freshly ground black pepper

Preheat the oven to 325°F.

Trim the crusts from the bread and cut into ½-inch cubes. Transfer to a large roasting pan and bake for about 15 minutes, shaking and stirring occasionally, until dry.

Meanwhile, heat the oil and butter in a large frying or sauté pan and add the bacon (if using), onion, and celery. Cook over a low–medium heat, stirring occasionally, for about 10 minutes, or until the vegetables have softened.

Transfer the toasted bread cubes to a large mixing bowl. Mix through the cranberries, pecans, herbs, and orange zest. Pour over the onion mixture and combine well with a large metal spoon until evenly mixed. Add the potato flour and a good seasoning of salt and pepper and mix well. Add the beaten eggs and stir until combined—the eggs need to be evenly mixed. Taste and add more seasoning, if necessary.

Spoon the mixture into a regular 12-cup muffin pan and transfer to the oven. Bake for 15 to 20 minutes, or until golden and crisp. Leave in the pan for 5 minutes before serving.

> ## TIP
> These little cups can be made ahead of time and frozen. Any leftovers can also be frozen. Bake from frozen for 10 to 15 minutes, or until warmed through.

# JAPANESE VEGETABLE TEMPURA

## WITH DIPPING SAUCE

You can use pretty much whatever vegetables you like for tempura—just as long as they will hold their shape in the hot oil. I use a mix (about 4 ounces each) of firm vegetables: thinly sliced sweet potato and zucchini, halved lengthways asparagus and green beans, red or green peppers, cut into thin strips and thinly sliced broccoli or cauliflower. The crunch of the batter and the freshness of the vegetable make this dish seem slightly naughty, yet you still have all the vitamins. You can serve this with an Asian dipping sauce in small bowls and provide a side of grated fresh ginger (or wasabi) to mix into the sauce, if desired.

## SERVES 4

vegetables of your choice—
    see recipe intro—cut into
    thin, bitesized pieces

4 cups sunflower (or other
    vegetable oil), for frying

### FOR THE BATTER

¼ cup potato flour

¼ cup fine rice flour

1 large free-range egg,
    beaten

sparkling water, chilled

### FOR THE DIPPING SAUCE

1 tablespoon dashi granules

4 tablespoons mirin
    (Japanese sweet wine)

2 tablespoons tamari

Make the dipping sauce by bringing 1 cup water to the boil in a small saucepan. Add the dashi and cook, stirring for 2 minutes. Remove from the heat and stir in the mirin and tamari.

Prepare the vegetables and heat the oil in a saucepan over a medium heat.

Meanwhile, make the batter by mixing the flours in a bowl. Pour the beaten egg into a measuring cup and add enough of the chilled water to come up to ¾ cup. Whisk into the flours until smooth.

Test if the oil is hot enough (350°F) by dropping a pinch of flour into the pan. It should bubble when dropped into the oil.

Using tongs, dip some of the vegetables into the batter, then quickly and carefully drop into the hot oil, taking care not to overfill the pan. Fry the vegetables, moving them around, so they cook evenly and become crisp and lightly colored. Remove with a slotted spoon and transfer to paper towels. Repeat with the remaining vegetables, ensuring the batter is well mixed before adding any more as the flour tends to sink to the bottom.

Serve with the dipping sauce.

## INGREDIENT NOTE

*Dashi is a great Japanese ingredient. It's a kind of stock, and provides an intense umami flavor. As well as being used in saiuces and soups (it forms the basis of the famous miso soup), dashi granules can be mixed into flours for a flavor hit.*

*Mirin is another essential Japanese condiment. Like sake, it is a rice wine, but less alcoholic. It's great with fish and is used in Teriyaki sauce. It's a good alternative to soy.*

# WHAT NANA TAUGHT ME:
# LAUGH, LOVE, EAT WELL . . .
# AND ENTERTAIN!

I learned many of my greatest lessons about cooking, entertaining, and just life in general from my nana. When I would ask her what she had cooked at the many dinner parties she had hosted over the years, she might recall a roast here or a dessert there, but a lot of the menus had blended together in her mind over time. Overall, she said that the food didn't really matter—she had her favorites, of course—but what she remembered was the company, the fun.

And therein lies the greatest wisdom when it comes to entertaining: the food is important, but not nearly as much as the people you enjoy it with. That doesn't mean I advocate not caring about the food—far from it—but at the end of the day, it doesn't matter whether you tried to make sole meunière or did a simple roast chicken, because it's the experience as a whole that makes a lasting impression. And that really takes off a huge amount of pressure.

I think people often shy away from entertaining because it can be intimidating—they don't know what to make, whom to invite, or they are worried it won't be any good. So I want to share here the most important lessons I learned from my grandmother, to help make the experience as easy and stress-free as possible.

# NANA'S TOP
# TIPS FOR
# ENTERTAINING

## FIND A REPERTOIRE THAT WORKS FOR YOU AND STICK TO IT

It's always good to develop that solid core list of dishes that are not too difficult or time consuming and that you know are crowd pleasers. The more often you make the dishes from this repertoire, the more confident you become with them. And that confidence gives you space to get more inventive with the sides or the dessert.

## DON'T TRY AND MASTER PERFECTLY COOKED SEA BASS FOR 10 PEOPLE

A lot of the dinners my nana entertained with were either roasts or stews. It is much easier if your meal centerpiece is either a single cut of meat that can be thrown into the oven with minimal interference or a braised or stewed dish, like short rib or beef bourguignon that can even be made a day ahead. What is the point of being stressed and stuck slaving away in the kitchen, unable to relax when you should be having fun with your guests?

## DON'T TAKE IT PERSONALLY.

Everyone has different tastes and some things are just not for everyone. Don't let that stop you from making the foods you like and enjoy.

## MAKE MISTAKES—AND LAUGH ABOUT THEM!

Probably the most important thing I learned about cooking from Nana was to feel comfortable in the kitchen, and not to be afraid of making mistakes. Some of my most memorable kitchen experiences are the blunders. And you know what? Those are some of my favorite memories because, looking back, they are so absurd and hilarious. After all, what is the worst that can happen?

## DON'T SWEAT THE SMALL STUFF—BUY IT

Not every single thing has to be made from scratch. There are so many high-quality products out there that can take such a weight off your shoulders. Will anyone ever know—or care—that you used pre-grated carrots in your carrot cake or that the mushrooms were pre-sliced?

## TRY NOT TO SPREAD OUT YOUR WORKSPACE

My grandmother learned this from cooking in her very small, very old kitchen in Hampstead. Somehow she managed to entertain from there.

## DON'T BE AFRAID TO ASK FOR HELP

Often, when cooking a dinner and hosting, we feel like we have to do everything and that's what leads to being overwhelmed. Having a little help with the washing up makes the situation so much more manageable and takes a huge weight off.

## ABUNDANCE MAKES PEOPLE FEEL SPECIAL

To throw a good party is to offer generosity to all your guests. You don't need to make thousands of different dishes; you just need to pick a menu that tastes great—and lots of it! A large platter filled with crushed ice and a freshly dressed crab, large pink juicy shrimp, bowls of aioli with chunks of bright yellow lemons scattered across a bed of deep green salty sea beans will look amazing and really won't cost the earth. Always pile it high—as high as your wallet will allow. There is nothing worse than a party that runs out of everything.

## PREP, PREP, AND PREP AGAIN

Preparation is everything. Design a menu which can, in the large part, be made in advance. The last thing you want is to be the host or hostess whose face is dripping with sweat when their guests arrive! So prepare everything and anything you can the day before and get it in the refrigerator, ready to spruce up on the day.

## OPEN A BOTTLE OF WINE—ENJOY YOURSELF

Create an old-fashioned wine cocktail by adding white wine to soda with mint leaves and freshly squeezed lemon. Or make spirits like rum and vodka into punches, adding pomegranate or hibiscus flowers—you can be adventurous here with color and taste. Get the drinks flowing quickly. Prepared pitchers mean guests can help themselves and you don't need to be making gin and tonics for 20!

## MAKE IT PRETTY

Setting the table on your terrace or in your garden or living room for a party is a magical way to get the mood just right. Fresh flowers in small jars, whether from a florist or just picked from the garden, are a fabulous way to make things sing for a summer or spring event. Bare twigs, fresh rosemary, branches, and pine cones dressed with a bit of sparkle are great to use from October onwards, through all those dark winter months. You don't need matching cutlery or tableware—you can pick up some beautiful platters and bowls from flea markets for next to nothing. Stash them away in a cupboard and then pull them out for your party and hey presto! It will look like a prop stylist has popped in to set up your event. If you use linens, then take the time to iron them—it's so simple but it makes your guests feel like you care. And make sure you have enough chairs, enough glasses, and lots of water at the ready at all times.

# FEEDING
# THE SOUL

## COMFORT AND INDULGENCE

Nowadays, we all understand that fresh, nourishing food makes us look good and feel amazing. In my case, going gluten free saved me from years of stomach upsets and skin complaints. But I am also convinced that a little bit of what you crave does you good. Eating gluten free should not be a source of stress—and while I do believe that we have to listen to our bodies, and not eat the things that our gut doesn't like, with a little knowledge and skill, you can still indulge in your favorite cakes and treats.

At culinary school I learned to cook professionally, following complicated and meticulous recipes and methods in the Escoffier tradition. But when I cook at home, I add my soul to the mixing bowl. As well as flavor, texture, and preparation, cooking, for me, means care and love and putting my heart into my work.

When I turned gluten free I was terrified that I would no longer be able to cook for everyone—to offer solace through my kitchen. Wanting to cook for friends and family became the driving force behind my working out how to recreate all their favorite dishes in gluten-free versions. Some of the recipes in this section are among my earliest creations. Raspberry Almond Shortbread Cookies (see page 129) were one of the very first things I baked at the age of 12, and one of the first recipes I converted to gluten free. Equally, my Chocolate Coconut Crinkles (see page 121) are one of my signature cookies. You can read all about my darling Nana and her apple pie recipe (see page 145–146), which fills me with so many memories. And, of course, there are all the breads. Missing bread was another major incentive for learning to cook gluten free, and so there is a good range of recipes in here: from Classic White and Gluten-Free Brown Bread (see pp. 169 and 170), to French Baguette and Brioche (see pp. 174 and 182), to Za'atar Flatbread (see page 173) and everything in between. This section is also packed with those naughty but essential treats, like crispy Fried Calamari with Aioli (see page 112), as well as lots of delicious desserts that I have picked up on my travels to France, England, and Italy as well as a few American classics.

My philosophy has always been to be honest with myself. I am conscious of what I eat, and I try to eat healthily 80 per cent of the time. But every now and again our bodies demand a gooey mac and cheese or some hot fried chicken. And I refuse to beat myself up for loving pizza or having a cocktail. So while I don't advocate eating from this section of the book every day, we all like to stay home with a box set and a plate of cookies every so often, and I am the first to put my hand up for that pleasure—with no guilt whatsoever!

# MY GORGEOUS MAC AND CHEESE
## (WITH TRUFFLE BUTTER)

This is one of my all-time favorite comfort foods. The warm, gooey, creamy texture, the cheese with just a hint of butter—all blended into one of the most sublime foods humankind has ever created. Mac and cheese also holds a special significance for me because it was the first dish I learned to cook all by myself. Making it gluten free simply requires using gluten-free pasta. I prefer brands such as Jovial and also Ancient Harvest quinoa. My one concession to occasionally making this a "fancy" mac and cheese, when the urge for decadence comes, is to melt a tablespoon or two of truffle butter into the sauce, right before serving. Totally delish.

## SERVES 4 TO 6

- 12 ounces gluten-free dried pasta
- 2 cups whole milk
- 3 tablespoons cornstarch (made into a slurry with 2 tablespoons water)
- 8 ounces Cheddar, grated
- 8 ounces Gruyère cheese, grated
- pinch of grated nutmeg
- pinch of cayenne pepper
- 1 teaspoon salt
- ½ teaspoon freshly ground black pepper
- 1 tablespoon truffle butter (optional)
- ½ stick butter, cubed
- ½ cup gluten-free breadcrumbs
- ½ cup Parmesan, finely grated

Preheat the oven to 350°F.

Bring a large saucepan of salted water to the boil. Drop the pasta carefully into the boiling water and simmer for 5 to 6 minutes. As with all gluten-free pasta, it is very important to cook it al dente, as it is more delicate and can get limp and droopy. Drain fully and refresh in cold water, then transfer to a baking dish about 8 x 10 x 2 inches.

Warm the milk over a medium heat and then add the cornstarch slurry, bit by bit, until the sauce thickens. Bring to the boil, then simmer for 1 to 2 minutes and whisk out any lumps. Reduce the heat and add the grated Cheddar and gruyère cheese. Add the nutmeg, cayenne, and salt and pepper and stir (with a wooden spoon) until creamy. (If you are dressing this dish up and are using truffle butter, melt this into the sauce now.) Add the cheese sauce to the baking dish and mix, fully coating the pasta.

In a separate saucepan, melt the butter with the gluten-free breadcrumbs over a low heat.

Remove from the heat. Add the Parmesan and mix together, making a crumble-style consistency and scatter across the top of the pasta. Bake for 20 to 25 minutes, until bubbling and golden brown.

# GNOCCHI

## WITH SICILIAN PISTACHIO PESTO

Pasta purists would only have you serve pesto with a long pasta like spaghetti. I love pesto with pretty much any pasta, and as gnocchi is made from potato, there is no gluten to worry about. Covered with Pecorino and Parmesan and served with a green salad, this is just one of my favorite lunch dishes for friends. And if you can get Sicilian pistachios, then do try, as they are the best. But of course, any good pistachios will do… I won't tell. Promise!

## SERVES 6 TO 8

1½ cups unsalted shelled pistachios

1 cup extra virgin olive oil, plus extra for storing pesto

1 garlic clove, mashed

½ cup Pecorino cheese, plus extra to serve

½ cup Parmesan, plus extra to serve

3 tablespoons chopped basil

2 tablespoons chopped mint

3 pounds gluten-free dried gnocchi (De Cecco is one of the best)

freshly ground black pepper

In a food processor, blitz the pistachios, oil, garlic, cheeses, and herbs into a pesto paste with some texture, adding a splash of water if needed.

Boil the gnocchi in salted water for 2 to 3 minutes or according to the package instructions. Drain, reserving some of the cooking water.

Stir the pesto into the gnocchi, adding a little of the reserved cooking water to help the pesto fully coat it. (You can store any leftover pesto. Simply transfer it to a jar or plastic container. Pour a thin layer of oil over the top of the pesto, close the container, and keep in the refrigerator for up to 5 days.)

Serve sprinkled with lots of grated Parmesan and Pecorino cheese and black pepper.

## TIP

*If you don't have any Pecorino cheese, just use all Parmesan cheese. You can also replace the mint with extra basil, if you prefer.*

# TRUFFLE RISOTTO

## WITH PARMESAN BROTH

This is such a fabulously rich and creamy dish, and although it's pretty simple to make, it does need your attention throughout the process, as you must keep stirring. But it is most definitely worth it.

I know Arborio has become the go-to risotto rice, but I urge you to ditch it and use carnaroli instead. It's so much lighter. And if you can get fresh truffle, it really makes this dish something very special. However, you can always use truffle butter, which is, of course, much cheaper and easier to find out of season and still works well.

## SERVES 4

### FOR THE PARMESAN BROTH

2 shallots, peeled and halved

1 head of garlic, halved

1 tablespoon vegetable oil

1 bay leaf

a few sprigs parsley

a few sprigs thyme

5 to 6 black peppercorns, whole

1 pound Parmesan

1 cup white wine

### FOR THE RISOTTO

1 small onion, finely chopped

1 tablespoon olive oil

2 cups carnaroli rice

1 cup white wine

4 to 6 cups Parmesan broth

½ tablespoon fresh white truffle, sliced or grated (or 3½ ounces black truffle butter, cut into cubes)

½ cup grated Parmesan, to serve

Begin by making the broth: in a large saucepan, sauté the shallots and garlic head in the vegetable oil, until golden. Add the bay leaf, parsley, thyme and peppercorns, the block of Parmesan, white wine, and 8 cups of water. Reduce by half (stirring regularly); this will take around 1½ to 2 hours. Strain and set aside. It should yield roughly 6 cups of broth.

To make the risotto, sauté the onion in olive oil over a medium heat until soft. Add the rice and coat in oil. Add the white wine and reduce in the pan, then gradually add the Parmesan broth by the ladleful, allowing it to be absorbed until the rice is cooked and produces a creamy risotto. Add the sliced truffle (or cubes of truffle butter). Serve with grated Parmesan.

# HALLOUMI FRIES

## WITH HARISSA YOGURT

The heat of the harissa (which you can find in most supermarkets) goes so well with the saltiness of the halloumi and the flavor of the za'atar. I tend to eat halloumi quite a lot, as it has the sort of meaty, chewy texture I sometimes crave when I am being a part-time veggie. I sometimes sprinkle pomegranate seeds onto the harissa yogurt, which adds a little sweet note to this dish.

## SERVES 6

1 tablespoon harissa paste

6 ounces Greek yogurt

1 tablespoon pomegranate seeds (optional)

2 (9 ounce) blocks halloumi cheese

3 tablespoons za'atar, plus extra for sprinkling

2 tablespoons gluten-free all-purpose flour

vegetable oil, for frying

To make the dip, mix the harissa with the yogurt. Sprinkle with pomegranate seeds, if using, and set aside.

For the fries, fill a deep-sided pan or wok with 2 inches oil and heat to 325°F. (Use a thermometer to keep the temperature constant.)

Cut each block of halloumi into 12 chunky fries, so you have 24 in total. Mix the za'atar with the flour in a wide, shallow bowl, then toss the halloumi pieces into the mixture.

Lower the fries into the hot oil with a slotted spoon and fry in batches for 2 to 3 minutes, until golden. Lift onto paper towels to absorb any excess oil, then transfer to a warm serving plate. Sprinkle with a little extra za'atar and serve with the harissa dip.

## INGREDIENT NOTE

*I first tasted harissa in North Africa. It's usually made from chiles, garlic, and herbs including coriander, smoked paprika, and caraway seeds. It is often mixed with water or tomato paste or juice and added to stews, tagines, and soups to give a good hearty kick. In Morocco I also had it served with olive oil as a spicy condiment. It usually comes in a paste or powder, to which you add oil and garlic.*

# FRIED CALAMARI

## WITH AIOLI

What can I say about this dish except YUM! This just takes me straight to holiday mode—even if it's the middle of winter and I am in the center of Manhattan.

The cornmeal here gives the dish a crunch. I serve mine with the fabulous Spanish condiment aioli—a garlic mayonnaise that makes all other condiments weep with envy.

## SERVES 2 TO 4

4 medium-sized calamari (squid), cleaned

4 tablespoons cornstarch

4 tablespoons gluten-free plain flour

2 tablespoons fine cornmeal or polenta

1 teaspoon sea salt

sunflower oil, for frying

3 tablespoons roughly chopped flat-leaf parsley

1 small red chile, seeded and chopped

lemon wedges, to serve

freshly ground black pepper

### FOR THE AIOLI

3 free-range egg yolks

4 garlic cloves

juice of ½ a lemon

pinch of sea salt

pinch of freshly ground black pepper

¼ cup extra virgin olive oil

¼ cup vegetable oil

mustard powder (optional)

saffron (optional)

Lightly pat the calamari dry with paper towels—don't completely dry them as they need some moisture for the flour to adhere. Slice the calamari bodies into rings, about ¼ inch in diameter.

When you're ready to cook, combine the flours, cornmeal, and salt in a shallow dish. Season with a little freshly ground black pepper. Fill a large, heavy-based saucepan or deep frying pan one third full with oil and heat over a medium-high heat, until a pinch of flour sizzles when it hits the oil.

Place a handful of the calamari in the flour mixture and shake off the excess. (It's important to dust with flour just before cooking, rather than trying to do it ahead.) Fry in batches for 1 to 2 minutes, until crisp and slightly golden. Remove from the pan using a slotted spoon, and place on paper towels. Sprinkle with salt, and then repeat with the remaining calamari rings.

To make the aioli, blend the egg yolks, garlic, lemon juice, salt, and pepper in a blender. Pour the oil into the blender in a steady stream, until you have a thick sauce. The mixture, once blended, should be vibrant and yellow in color. To vary the flavor, you can add a little mustard or some saffron. If you'd like your aioli runnier, add a couple of tablespoons of hot water.

Toss the cooked calamari with the parsley and chile, and serve with lemon wedges and the aioli. Instant holiday feeling.

# CLASSIC AMERICAN MEATBALLS

## WITH FRENCH BAGUETTE

This dish takes me straight back to my childhood. Meatballs and spaghetti, loaded with Parmesan, was our Friday night treat after school. I still love these with gluten-free pasta, but for a weekend lunch or kitchen supper they work perfectly with my freshly baked baguette and a green salad. I use a pork and beef mix in this recipe, but if you don't eat pork you can easily use just beef instead.

## SERVES 6

### FOR THE MEATBALLS
2 cups ground pork
2 cups ground beef
1 large free-range egg
1 tablespoon finely chopped
    flat-leaf parsley
1 tablespoon finely chopped
    oregano
1 garlic clove, minced
½ cup gluten-free breadcrumbs
2 ounces Parmesan, finely grated
sea salt and freshly ground
    black pepper
sunflower oil, for frying

### FOR THE TOMATO SAUCE
2 onions, peeled and diced
2 tablespoons olive oil
1 garlic clove, crushed
2 (14 ounce) cans whole
    tomatoes
I tablespoon tomato purée
½ teaspoon sea salt
½ teaspoon granulated sugar
¼ cup butter, cubed

To make the meatballs, mix together all the ingredients except the oil in a bowl. Form the mixture into balls, using your hands. It should make around 18 to 20 meatballs.

Brown the meatballs in sunflower oil in a heavy-based saucepan over a medium heat for 4 to 5 minutes and set aside.

For the sauce, in a separate saucepan, sauté the onions in the oil until soft, then add the garlic and soften. Add the tomatoes and tomato pureé, bring to the boil, and simmer over a low heat until reduced and softened. Add the salt, butter, and sugar, and set aside to cool. Transfer to a food processor and blitz to a purée.

Place the meatballs and the tomato sauce in a heavy-based saucepan and simmer over medium heat for 30 minutes.

Serve with a warm gluten-free baguette (see page 174) and a mixed green salad.

# BUTTERMILK FRIED CHICKEN

One of the great contributions of the USA to world cuisine has to be fried chicken. The other is serving the chicken with waffles (see my Gloriously Gluten-free Waffles, page 31) to create one of the most addictive and satisfying combos imaginable. Fried chicken is such an utterly simple dish when cooked right. There's a reason why it gets sold by the bucket! In my gluten-free version I have added cornmeal for flavor and texture, and I find the blend of garlic, paprika, cayenne, salt, and pepper works a treat. Who needs the Colonel's secret recipe anyway?

## SERVES 4

6 to 8 skinless chicken pieces (to include a mixture of thighs, drumsticks and small breasts, depending on your favorite cuts)

2 cups buttermilk (you can use dairy or almond milk with 2 tablespoons of lemon juice added)

1 teaspoon cayenne pepper

1 teaspoon paprika

1 teaspoon coarse sea salt

½ teaspoon freshly ground black pepper

½ teaspoon garlic powder

½ cup cornmeal or polenta

1 cup all-purpose gluten-free flour

canola oil, for frying

Preheat the oven to 400°F.

Soak the chicken pieces in the buttermilk for 1 to 2 hours in the refrigerator to tenderize them.

Place all the dry ingredients in a bowl and mix. Drain the chicken, then coat it in the flour mixture, rolling each piece in it twice to ensure full coverage.

If you don't have a deep-fat fryer, then fill a heavy-based pot with at least 3 to 4 inches of canola oil and fry 1 or 2 pieces at a time at 350°F for 6 minutes. (It's important to keep the temperature constant by using a thermometer.)

Remove the cooked chicken from the oil, using a slotted spoon, and place on a baking sheet. Finish cooking in the oven for 12 to 18 minutes (depending on the size and cut of the portion) to ensure maximum crispness.

Drain off any excess oil on a rack and devour.

# MARGHERITA PIZZA

## WITH BASIL AND MOZZARELLA

Does anything say a few friends round for a chilled-out evening more than pizza? Chewy, crisp crust, just enough sweet acidic tomato sauce, topped with gooey mozzarella, a few herbs, and maybe a few slices of chorizo or good salami. It's loved all over the world for a very good reason. It was one of the hardest things for me to give up and so one of the first that I tried to recreate gluten free.

Having grown up in New York, I consider myself to have very high standards when it comes to pizza, but most of the gluten-free options I found tasted of cardboard. Luckily, things have changed, and these days even Domino's make a gluten-free version. But making your own can never be beaten. The dough can be a bit sticky and messy, but don't worry about that. Once you get your dough down pat, you will wonder why you never made your own before.

---

## MAKES 4 PIZZAS

### FOR THE PIZZA BASE

4 cups gluten-free Caputo Fiore Glut flour (available on Amazon if you can't find it locally)

½ teaspoon instant yeast

2½ teaspoons coarse sea salt

1½ tablespoons extra virgin olive oil, plus extra for oiling

1½ cups warm water

rice flour, for dusting

cornmeal, for dusting

To make the pizza base, put the flour, yeast, salt, and oil in a stand mixer and mix with the dough hook attachment to combine. Gradually add the warm water with the mixer still running until the ingredients come together.

Stop the mixer, scrape down the sides of the bowl, and then put the mixer on high speed for 2 to 3 minutes. The dough will appear sticky and quite wet. Unlike traditional dough, this does not need a lot of kneading as there is no gluten to develop, so scrape it onto a surface dusted with rice flour and lightly pat/knead, until you have a smooth ball of dough.

Lightly oil the dough ball, cover in plastic wrap and place in a plastic container (also lightly oiled). Refrigerate overnight.

The following day, preheat the oven to the highest setting (at least 425°F). If you have a 9-inch pizza stone, this is the time to use it! Place the stone in the oven to preheat as the oven heats up.

Remove the dough from the refrigerator and bring it back to room temperature (for at least 1 hour).

## FOR THE TOPPING

1 (14-ounce) can whole Italian tomatoes (San Marzano, ideally), chopped

pinch of salt

1 to 2 tablespoons extra virgin olive oil, plus extra for drizzling

1 garlic clove, minced

½ teaspoon dried oregano

10 basil leaves, torn

2 balls buffalo mozzarella, torn

Meanwhile, make the topping. In a bowl, mix together the tomatoes, salt, olive oil, garlic, and oregano.

Divide the pizza dough into 4 balls and roll each out into a pizza-base round. It is best to cook one pizza at a time. Transfer the base to a pizza peel or a baking sheet dusted with cornmeal.

Spread a thin layer of tomato topping over the pizza base, leaving a lip around the edge. Scatter with basil leaves and mozzarella and drizzle with extra virgin olive oil.

Use the pizza peel or dusted baking sheet to transfer the base directly onto the pizza stone. The stone must stay in the oven (and should remain in the oven to cool as well—never touch a hot pizza stone).

Cook for 10 to 12 minutes, until the cheese is melted, the pizza crust is golden brown and the base is fully cooked. Use the pizza peel or dusted baking sheet to remove the pizza from the stone.

Repeat with the remaining bases and toppings.

## TIP

*To achieve a crips base, it is important to have your oven preheated to its highest setting. Your pizza stone or baking sheet should also be preheated.*

# SWEET LEMON POPPY SEED BARS

This has all the flavors and textures of a classic pie but I find making it into bars means that I don't wolf the whole thing down in one sitting. I think this was possibly what tea was made for as it's the absolute all-time teatime treat. The poppy seed was once thought to offer magical powers of invisibility, which is exactly what happens every time I make these bars—they vanish!

## MAKES 16 SQUARES

### FOR THE CRUST
1½ unsalted butter, softened
¼ cup superfine sugar
2 cups gluten-free all-purpose flour
¼ teaspoon sea salt
1½ tablespoons poppy seeds
grated zest of 1 lemon

### FOR THE FILLING
4 large free-range eggs
1½ superfine sugar
¼ teaspoon salt
finely grated zest of 2 lemons
½ cup lemon juice

### TO FINISH
2 to 3 tablespoons confectioner's sugar

Preheat the oven to 350°F.

Line an 8-inch square baking pan with parchment paper.

For the crust, beat the butter and sugar together in a stand mixer until light and fluffy. Add the flour, salt, poppy seeds, and lemon zest and mix again, until well combined and you have a soft dough. Press the mixture into the base of the prepared baking pan, then chill in the freezer for around 15 minutes. Transfer to the oven and bake into a crust for 18 to 20 minutes.

For the filling, beat the eggs in a bowl. Add the sugar, salt, lemon zest, and juice. Pour the mixture over the crust and bake for 30 to 35 minutes, until set. Remove from the oven and leave to cool completely.

Cut into squares, dust with confectioner's sugar and serve. These bars can be stored in an airtight container in the refrigerator for up to 3 days.

# CANDIED FLORENTINES

These are just such a delight to eat and so easy to make. They're also perfect for storing for a couple of weeks in an airtight container for a little teatime treat. I don't tend to dip my Florentines in chocolate, but if you can't live without the chocolate base, then simply melt some dark chocolate in a bain-marie (a small bowl set over a saucepan of simmering water – but don't allow the bottom of the bowl to touch the water), dip each biscuit into the chocolate, and set aside on a rack to cool and harden. You can use a fork when the chocolate is still soft to make the traditional markings.

## MAKES 15

3 tablespoons unsalted butter

⅓ cup demerara sugar

1 tablespoon heavy cream

pinch of salt

2 tablespoons gluten-free all-purpose flour

2 tablespoons hazelnuts, roughly chopped

½ cup sliced almonds

1 tablespoon candied ginger, finely chopped

⅓ cup candied peel, chopped

⅓ cup glacé cherries, chopped to similar size as peel

1 cup gluten-free dark chocolate (optional)

Preheat the oven to 350°F.

Grease 2 large baking sheets and cover with parchment paper.

In a heavy-based saucepan set over a medium heat, melt the butter and sugar until fully combined and the sugar has dissolved.

Remove from the heat and stir in the cream and salt to make a caramel mixture.

Sift the flour into a bowl and then add the nuts, ginger, candied peel, and cherries and mix until coated with flour. Add the fruit and nuts to the cream mixture and combine.

Spoon a heaped teaspoon of the mixture onto the baking sheet and flatten with the back of a spoon. Make sure to leave enough space, as the Florentines will spread as they bake.

Bake for 10 to 12 minutes, until golden brown. Remove from the oven and leave to cool and set.

If decorating with dark chocolate, remove the Florentines from the baking sheets and, once completely cold, dip in melted chocolate and place on cooling rack to set.

# CHOCOLATE COCONUT CRINKLES

So, I suppose if there was one recipe that really began my whole gluten-free journey, it would be these little cookies. I have been making these since I was about four foot tall and these were one of the first recipes I made gluten free, so if you like, they are my little gluten-free guinea pigs—oh and they also taste divine. If you have an open can of coconut milk then you can use that instead of dairy milk for even more coconut flavor.

## MAKES 30

4 ounces good-quality gluten-free dark chocolate, 50 to 70% cocoa solids, chopped

½ cup coconut oil, semi-softened

1½ cups lightly packed light brown sugar

1½ cups gluten-free all-purpose flour

⅓ cup ground almonds or ground hazelnuts

⅓ cup unsweetened cocoa powder

2 teaspoons gluten-free baking powder

¾ teaspoon sea salt

2 free-range eggs, beaten

3 tablepoons milk (dairy or coconut)

2 teaspoons vanilla extract or vanilla paste

### TO COAT

¼ cup granulated sugar

⅓ cup confectioner's sugar

Melt the chocolate in a bain-marie (place a glass bowl over a pan of steaming water, but make sure the bottom of the bowl doesn't touch the water as it will scorch the chocolate). Stir occasionally until melted. Set aside.

Beat the coconut oil and light brown sugar on high speed with an electric stand mixer for about 3 minutes until smooth.

Meanwhile, sift together the gluten-free flour, ground almonds or hazelnuts, cocoa powder, baking powder, and salt in a bowl.

Turn the mixer to low speed and add the eggs, one at a time. Still on low, add the melted chocolate. Then add the milk and vanilla and beat until smooth. With the mixer still on low, slowly add the flour mixture and mix until just combined.

Transfer the dough to a non-metal bowl and cover with plastic wrap, placed directly on the top of the dough. Refrigerate for at least 1 hour (preferably 2 to 3 hours), until the dough becomes very solid, almost like a ganache. This dough can easily be made the night before and refrigerated until needed.

Preheat the oven to 350°F and line two baking sheets with parchment paper. Put the granulated sugar in a small bowl and the confectioner's sugar in another. Using a mini ice-cream scoop or a spoon, scoop out the ganache-like dough, and roll into balls, about the size of a large marble. Coat each ball in granulated sugar and then confectioner's sugar, making sure there is a good coating of confectioner's sugar on the ball.

Place on the prepared baking sheets, then gently flatten each ball with the palm of your hand or the back of a spoon. Bake for 12 to 15 minutes, or until risen, cracked, and just firm to the touch. Leave to cool on the trays for 5 minutes, then transfer to a wire rack to cool completely. These will keep for 7 days in an airtight container.

# HONEY ALMOND TRUFFLES

I love to have a little bowl of these truffles in my refrigerator at all times. Made with almonds and prunes and my beloved dark chocolate, one or two of these will give you an instant hit of sweetness, but not at the expense of your waistline. You can use different toppings—mini chocolate chips, hand-chopped roasted almonds, freeze-dried strawberries, and shaved chocolate are just a few ideas.

## MAKES 24

¾ cup blanched almonds

7 ounces soft pitted prunes (about 27), roughly chopped

2 tablespoons almond butter (smooth or crunchy)

2 tablespoons honey

1 tablespoon confectioner's sugar

3 tablespoons cocoa powder

5 ounces good-quality gluten-free dark chocolate, 70% cocoa solids, broken into pieces

2 to 3 tablespoons sliced almonds, to decorate

Preheat the oven to 400°F.

Toast the almonds by placing them on a tray and roasting in the oven for about 10 minutes, or until a pale golden color.

Transfer the toasted almonds and the prunes to a food processor and blitz until combined and the nuts are chopped. Add the almond butter, honey, sugar, and cocoa powder and pulse until well mixed. Transfer the mixture to a bowl and chill in the refrigerator for 30 minutes.

Line a baking sheet with parchment paper. Roll the mixture into balls (about a tablespoonful per ball—each ball should be about ¾-inch in diameter) and place onto the prepared tray. Chill in the refrigerator for 15 minutes.

Melt the chocolate in a bain-marie (a small bowl set over a saucepan of simmering water – but don't allow the bottom of the bowl to touch the water), stirring occasionally, until melted. Using a skewer or toothpick, dip each of the chilled balls into the melted chocolate. Allow any excess chocolate to drip off and then return the truffles to the baking sheet. Sprinkle the tops with a few sliced almonds. Refrigerate until needed. These will keep in a sealed containter in the refrigerator for up to 10 days.

# VANILLA MADELEINES

Madeleines are such a classic treat—so, so elegant, and so very French. I actually bought my madeleine pan when I was in France, which is, perhaps, a strange souvenir—but hey, kitchen geek alert! And I'm proud to this day that my madeleines come out of the most authentic pan I could get my hands on.

When I first posted these on Instagram and my other social channels, I wasn't sure how they'd be received, as they are quite a discreet little cake, but everyone went mad for them and I'm always being asked for my recipe… so here it is. Ooh la la, indeed.

## MAKES 18 MADELEINES (OR 10 MINI MUFFINS)

1 stick soft unsalted butter, plus extra for greasing

¾ cup gluten-free all-purpose flour, plus extra for dusting

½ cup superfine sugar, plus extra for dusting

2 medium free-range eggs

1 teaspoon vanilla extract

1 teaspoon gluten-free baking powder

½ cup ground almonds

pinch of sea salt

confectioner's sugar, for dusting

Preheat the oven to 350°F.

Grease a madeleine pan (or a mini-muffin pan) with plenty of butter and dust with flour.

Put all the ingredients in a large bowl and beat until just combined. Divide the batter between the pans, using about 1 tablespoon for each of the madeleine cups, or two-thirds full for each of the mini-muffin cups. Save any remaining batter and reuse the current madeleine pan once emptied and cooled.

Bake for 10 to 12 minutes until firm and golden (the mini muffins will take 15 minutes).

Remove from the oven and leave to stand for a minute or two. Run a knife around the edges, remove, and place on a wire rack to cool completely. Dust with superfine or confectioner's sugar to serve.

## TIP

*A lemon glaze makes a wonderful addition to this recipe. Simply whisk together ¾ cup confectioner's sugar and 2 tablespoons lemon juice, then dip the top side of each madeleine into the glaze while warm and leave to cool and set.*

# BROWNIE CUPCAKES

## WITH TAHINI FROSTING

I must confess, despite their popularity, I was decidedly anti-cupcake for the longest time. (Maybe it stemmed from the time I had to make 500 of them for a birthday party!) It wasn't until I turned the dessert I've surely made most often in my life—the chocolate brownie—into cupcakes that I truly realized their potential.

I used to top these with a peanut butter frosting, but recently discovered that tahini is fresher and lighter. If you want to make these in mini cupcake tins, reduce the baking time to 10 minutes.

## MAKES 20

### FOR THE CUPCAKES

9 ounces gluten-free semi-sweet chocolate

6 ounces gluten-free unsweetened chocolate

1 cup coconut oil, melted and cooled

3 cups light brown sugar

1½ cups ground hazelnuts or ground almonds

¾ cup sorghum flour

1½ teaspoons fine sea salt

1½ teaspoons baking soda

6 large free-range eggs, beaten

3 tablespoons good-quality vanilla extract

### FOR THE FROSTING

8 tablespoons unsalted butter, at room temperature

⅔ cup tahini, well-stirred

½ cup confectioner's sugar, sifted

½ teaspoon fine sea salt

grated gluten-free chocolate, for sprinkling

Preheat the oven to 350°F and line two regular muffin pans with 20 paper cups.

Melt the chocolate in a bain-marie over a low heat (place a glass bowl over a pan of steaming water, but make sure the bottom of the bowl doesn't touch the water as it will scorch the chocolate). When the chocolate has melted, set aside to cool.

Combine the coconut oil with the cooled chocolate.

Whisk together the dry ingredients in a large mixing bowl. Add the eggs, vanilla, and the chocolate mixture and beat together for about 2 minutes, until the batter thickens and becomes glossy.

Divide the batter into the prepared pans, filling each case two-thirds.

Bake for 22 to 25 minutes. You want them to seem almost under-baked, so that they keep their soft and fudgy centers.

The tops will become cracked and fall, having risen, so don't panic... it's how it's meant to be! Leave the cupcakes to cool completely before frosting, otherwise it will slide straight off.

To make the frosting, place all the ingredients in a food processor and mix together until the butter has softened and the ingredients are fully combined. This is slightly thinner than the classic cupcake frosting. Swirl 1 to 2 teaspoons on top of each cupcake. Sprinkle over grated gluten-free chocolate to finish.

# TRULY SCRUMPTIOUS OATMEAL CHOCOLATE CHIP COOKIES

One of the most quintessentially American desserts has to be the chocolate chip cookie. It may be a humble dish, but few are more satisfying. I grew up making the recipe with pre-packaged dough— the instant gratification of being able to pop those cold lumps of dough into an oven for ten minutes and come up with warm, melty chocolate chip cookies trumped those store-bought ones every time.

I have used half brown and half white sugar in this recipe, as I find it gives a good flavor. Of course, it goes without saying that these cookies are incredible eaten warm, straight from the oven, but they also hold their soft, chewy texture for nearly a week after baking, stored in an airtight container. Some people may prefer a crisp cookie, but I've always loved the soft doughy, almost under-baked versions that take me straight back to my childhood.

## MAKES 18 TO 20

1 stick unsalted softened butter, cut into pieces

½ cup lightly packed light brown sugar

½ cup superfine sugar

1 free-range egg

1 cup gluten-free all-purpose flour

1½ cups rolled oats

½ teaspoon xanthan gum

½ teaspoon gluten-free baking powder

½ cup gluten-free dark (unsweetened) chocolate chips

1 teaspoon vanilla extract

Preheat the oven to 400°F. Line 2 baking sheets with parchment paper.

Beat the butter and sugars in an electric stand mixer for 3 to 4 minutes, or until well combined, scraping down the side of the bowl when needed. Add the egg and beat until incorporated.

Combine the flour, oats, xanthan gum, and baking powder. Add the flour mixture to the mixer, beating on a low speed until combined. Stir through the chocolate chips. Chill in the refrigerator, covered, for at least 30 minutes.

Using your hands, roll pieces of the chilled dough into ¾-inch balls and space about 2 inches apart on the prepared baking sheets (the cookies will spread while cooking). Bake for 9 to 12 minutes, or until golden. Leave on the sheets for 5 minutes before transferring to a wire rack to cool completely.

## TIP

*If you prefer crisp cookies, bake for closer to 12 minutes.*

# RASPBERRY ALMOND SHORTBREAD COOKIES

Shortbread cookies were always among my favorites growing up, and these were one of the first things, aged 12, I started baking on my own. When I went gluten free, I found my shortbread recipe was one of the easiest to convert. With the traditional butter, sugar, and eggs as the foundation, it is very easy to just substitute a gluten-free flour blend for the wheat flour. With my discovery of ground almonds, I found the perfect ingredient that even improved upon the original recipe. They remind me of the Austrian *linzer torte*, which is made with ground almonds and hazelnuts.

## MAKES 24

2 sticks unsalted butter, softened

½ teaspoon sea salt

¾ cup turbinado or demerara sugar

3 large free-range egg yolks

1 tablespoon vanilla extract

2 cups gluten-free all-purpose flour

½ teaspoon gluten-free baking powder

1 cup ground almonds

1 cup shredded coconut (optional)

1 cup raspberry jam

Preheat the oven to 375°F. Line a baking tray with parchment paper.

Cream the butter, salt, and sugar in an electric mixer until smooth, light, and fluffy. Slowly add the egg yolks and vanilla extract and mix until combined.

In a separate bowl, mix the flour mix and ground almonds together. With the mixer on low speed, add the flour mixture to the butter. Mix until the dough begins to come together and pulls away from the sides.

Scrape the dough from the bowl, flatten into a disc, and cover in plastic wrap. Chill in the refrigerator for 30 minutes. (You can also make the dough ahead of time and refrigerate overnight.)

Roll the dough into small balls, about a tablespoon in size. If you want to add some extra flavor and texture, roll the balls in shredded coconut.

Place the balls on the lined baking sheet and press an indentation into the top of each one. The cookies may seem small, but they will spread significantly in the oven. Spoon a little raspberry jam into each indentation—around ½ teaspoon for each.

Bake for 12 to 15 minutes until the edges are golden brown. Leave to cool on a wire rack. The cookies will have expanded quite a bit, so you may want to add some more raspberry jam—roughly ½ teaspoon—to the indentations, while they are cooling.

# CHOCOLATE ECLAIRS

This is certainly one for all you *British Baking Show* fans out there, as it's quite an advanced recipe. *Pâte à choux* is the classic French pastry dough—it's the only pastry dough that is cooked twice—first the milk, butter, and flour batter are cooked on the stovetop and then, once the eggs are added, the dough is baked in the oven. This unusual method of cooking is what gives the yellow, eggy dough its distinctive crisp, chewy crust and hollow center. There is no leavening in *pâte à choux* and the puffiness and hollow center are achieved purely by steam. Equally, crème pâtissière is a classic filling for the éclair—however, to simplify things you can replace this with a simpler option, by whisking together 1 cup heavy cream, 2 tablespoons confectioner's sugar, and a teaspoon of vanilla extract, until they form soft peaks.

## MAKES 12

### FOR THE PÂTE À CHOUX
6 tablespoons unsalted butter

1 tablespoon granulated sugar

1 teaspoon coarse sea salt

⅓ cup plus 2 tablespoons whole milk

⅓ cup plus 2 tablespoons water

1¼ cups flour (half superfine brown rice flour, a quarter superfine white rice flour, and a quarter tapioca starch)

¼ teaspoon gluten-free baking powder

3 extra-large free-range eggs

### FOR THE CRÈME PÂTISSIÈRE
2¼ cups whole milk

6 free-range egg yolks

⅔ cup granulated sugar

¼ cornstarch

1 vanilla pod, split lengthways

### FOR THE CHOCOLATE GLAZE
½ cup heavy cream

5 ounces gluten-free dark chocolate, finely chopped

Preheat the oven to 425°F.

Line 2 baking sheets with parchment paper or silicone mats.

Bring the butter, sugar, salt, milk, and water to the boil in a saucepan. Remove from the heat. Use a wooden spoon to quickly stir in the flour mixture and baking powder and beat until the mixture comes together to make a smooth, heavy dough. Return to a low heat and beat constantly for about 3 minutes until the mixture pulls away from the sides of the saucepan.

Remove from the heat and transfer the dough to the bowl of an electric stand mixer. Beat in the eggs, one at a time, mixing well until combined. When all the eggs have been added, the dough will be thick, smooth, and shiny.

Spoon the dough into a piping bag fitted with a ½-inch plain nozzle. Pipe twelve 4-inch lengths of dough onto the lined trays, spacing them 2 inches apart, so they have room to puff up as they bake. Sprinkle the sheet (but not the pastry) with a few drops of water, to create steam, and bake for 10 minutes. Reduce the oven temperature to 375°F and bake for a further 15 minutes, or until golden brown and crisp. Remove from the oven and transfer to a wire rack to cool. You can make these in advance and freeze them, thawing when required.

*Recipe continues overleaf*

To make the crème pâtissière, whisk together ½ cup of the milk, the egg yolks, half the sugar, and the cornstarch in a medium bowl.

Scrape the seeds from the vanilla pod. In a saucepan, heat the remaining milk with the vanilla pod, the scraped seeds and the remaining sugar over a medium heat. Let the sugar dissolve and bring to a simmer, without stirring.

Whisk the hot milk mixture once small bubbles begin to form, as it reaches a simmer. Gradually whisk the hot milk into the egg mixture. You don't have to worry about the eggs scrambling as the cornstarch prevents that. Return the egg and milk mixture to the saucepan and cook over a medium heat for 1 to 2 minutes, whisking constantly, until the mixture simmers and thickens.

Remove from the heat and discard the vanilla pod. Press some plastic wrap directly on top of the surface to prevent a skin from forming. Refrigerate until cold for 3 to 4 hours. The crème pâtissière can be made 3 days ahead and refrigerated.

When you are ready to fill the éclairs, transfer the crème pâtissière to a piping bag with a ¼-inch plain nozzle. Make a small hole in the base of each éclair with the nozzle and gently squirt in the filling.

For the chocolate glaze, heat the cream in a small saucepan until it begins to simmer. In a heatproof bowl, pour the cream over the chopped chocolate and leave to stand until the chocolate has melted. Stir until smooth.

Carefully dip the top side of the filled éclairs into the glaze. Let the excess drip off before transferring to a wire rack to let the glaze set.

# THE BEST BIRTHDAY CAKE IN THE WORLD

I've always been a total chocaholic. My tastes in chocolate have refined since childhood and I never cook (and rarely even eat!) less than 70% cacao now—once you get used to the less sweet taste, and the health benefits, I find you just don't want to go back. However, you might want to substitute a semi-sweet for high-cacao dark chocolate in this recipe if you aren't used to eating such super-rich chocolate. And you should check your chocolate's ingredient label, as some brands do have gluten in them.

This cake uses the ever-versatile ganache in two different ways: made with less cream and thickened in the refrigerator as a dense, rich filling between the two cake layers; and as a thinner, pourable, and molten glaze over the top, drizzling tantalizingly down the sides. This recipe has become my classic birthday cake and is a bit of a legend in its own lifetime.

## SERVES 12

### FOR THE CAKE

¾ cup gluten-free all-purpose flour, plus extra for dusting

14 ounces gluten-free dark (or semi-sweet) chocolate, chopped

¼ cup ground almonds

3 tablespoons cocoa powder

1 teaspoon gluten-free baking powder

½ teaspoon sea salt

1 stick unsalted butter

1 cup granulated sugar

4 medium free-range eggs

1 teaspoon vanilla extract

### FOR THE GANACHE FILLING

8 ounces gluten-free dark (or semi-sweet) chocolate, finely chopped

½ cup heavy cream

Preheat the oven to 350°F.

Grease two 8-inch cake pans and line the bases with circles of parchment paper. Dust with gluten-free flour and shake off any excess.

Melt the chocolate in a bain-marie (a bowl set over a pan of simmering water—be careful not to let the bowl touch the hot water as it will scorch the chocolate). Remove from the heat and leave to cool.

Whisk together the flour, ground almonds, cocoa powder, baking powder, and salt.

In the bowl of an electric stand mixer, cream together the butter and sugar until light and fluffy. Add the eggs, one at a time, and beat on high until they turn pale yellow and increase in volume. Turn the mixer on low and slowly pour in the melted chocolate and the vanilla extract. Add the flour mixture and beat gently, until just combined.

Divide the batter equally between the prepared cake pans and bake for 15 to 20 minutes, or until the cake starts to pull away from the sides and a skewer inserted in the center comes out clean. Leave to cool on a wire rack. The surface may crack slightly as it cools.

*Recipe continues overleaf*

## FOR THE GANACHE GLAZE

1½ cups heavy cream

6 ounces gluten-free dark (or semi-sweet) chocolate, finely chopped

While the cake is cooling, prepare the ganache filling. Put the chopped chocolate in a heatproof bowl. Heat the cream in a saucepan, until it is just starting to simmer, then immediately pour it over the chopped chocolate, stirring gently to combine. Leave to stand for a few minutes until the chocolate has melted. Stir to fully combine, until the ganache comes together in a creamy, silky mass. You can let it thicken at room temperature, which will take about an hour, or quicken the process by covering with plastic wrap and chilling in the refrigerator.

Place one of the cooled cakes top-side down on a cake plate. Spread the cooled chocolate ganache filling over it in a thick layer, then top with the remaining cake. Place in the refrigerator to allow the filling to solidify.

Meanwhile, make the glaze by heating the cream in a saucepan until just beginning to simmer. Pour the hot cream over the finely chopped chocolate in a glass bowl and stir to combine. Let the ganache glaze sit for a few minutes to allow the chocolate to melt completely. Stir until fully combined and silky in texture. Place in the refrigerator for 1 to 2 hours to reach a thicker consistency, which will enable it to cling to the cake.

Pour the silky ganache glaze slowly over the assembled cake, starting in the center and letting it gently spread over the sides, using a mini offset spatula to coat evenly.

This cake can be served immediately or refrigerated and eaten later, with the chocolate ganache thickening and infusing the entire cake into one decadent chocolatey whole. However, always allow the cake to return to room temperature before serving.

# COFFEE STREUSEL CAKE

I love the way this streusel cake has a hidden layer of crunchy yumminess tucked away in its middle—as if the crunchy layer on the top wasn't enough! A bit coffee, a bit nutty, a bit chocolatey—you can serve this cake with ice cream, as a dessert or as the perfect treat for a coffee meetup with friends.

## SERVES 8 TO 10

### FOR THE CAKE

1 tablespoon instant coffee powder

1 tablespoon boiling water

1½ sticks softened unsalted butter, cubed

¾ cup superfine sugar

3 free-range eggs, beaten

1½ cups gluten-free all-purpose flour

1 teaspoon gluten-free baking powder

pinch of sea salt

### FOR THE STREUSEL TOP

½ cup chopped walnuts or pecans

¼ cup demerara sugar

¼ cup gluten-free dark chocolate chips

Preheat the oven to 350°F.

Grease a loaf pan (about 8.5 x 4.5 inches) and line the base with parchment paper. Leave a little of the paper overhanging the pan, as this makes it easier to remove the cake when cool.

Make the streusel topping by combining all the ingredients in a small bowl and set aside.

To make the cake, dissolve the coffee in the boiling water. Place in an electric stand mixer with all of the remaining ingredients and mix on medium speed until just combined. Spoon half the cake batter into the prepared pan and sprinkle with half the streusel topping. Add the rest of the batter and sprinkle over the remaining topping.

Bake for 45 to 55 minutes, or until risen and firm to the touch (if the cake is browning too much during baking, cover the top with foil). Leave to cool in the pan.

Use the overhanging parchment paper to help lift the cake out of the pan. Store in an airtight container for up to 5 days.

# PISTACHIO NUT CAKE

## WITH BLOOD ORANGES

This nut cake works with most fruits—but I just love the tart citrusy orange, combined with the pistachios. If blood oranges aren't in season, then you can use standard oranges (see page 140) but just make sure they have thin skins.

Nut cakes are a great way to bake when you go gluten-free, and you can play around with different flour combinations. See pp. 14 to 16 to get ideas on which flours work for which recipes—ground almonds and chestnut flour are both great friends of the gluten-free baker. This recipe calls for pistachio paste—this can be bought online, or you can make your own by whizzing up 1 cup pistachios with 2 tablespoons coconut oil.

### SERVES 8

#### FOR THE CAKE

¾ cup unsalted pistachios, shelled

1½ cups all purpose gluten-free flour (see recipe intro)

grated zest of 1 blood orange

2 teaspoons gluten-free baking powder

1 teaspoon baking soda

¼ teaspoon sea salt

½ cup unsalted butter, at room temperature

¾ cup superfine sugar

¼ cup light muscovado sugar

3 medium free-range eggs

¼ cup pistachio paste (see recipe intro)

⅓ cup plain Greek or coconut yogurt

pinch of cardamom (optional)

¼ teaspoon orange blossom water (optional)

#### FOR THE SYRUP

½ cup superfine sugar

½ cup blood orange juice or freshly squeezed regular orange juice

Preheat the oven to 350°F. Grease and line the base of a 9-inch cake pan with parchment paper.

In a food processor, grind the pistachios until they are fine, making sure not to over-process to a paste. Add the flour, orange zest, baking powder, baking soda, and salt and gently pulse to combine.

In the bowl of an electric stand mixer, cream the butter and sugars until light and fluffy.

With the mixer set on low, add the eggs, one at a time. Then add the pistachio paste and yogurt and mix until incorporated.

If using, add the cardamom and/or orange blossom water, then slowly add the pistachio and flour mixture until the batter comes together. Scrape into the prepared cake pan and smooth the top.

Bake for 45 minutes (check the cake is cooked by popping a knife or skewer into the center—it's ready when it comes out clean and the top is browned). You can cover the cake with a layer of parchment if it appears to be browning too quickly.

For the syrup, combine the sugar and orange juice in a small saucepan over medium-low heat until the sugar is fully dissolved. Leave the liquid to gently bubble for a minute once the sugar has dissolved.

Using a toothpick, gently prick the top of the cake. Pour the warm syrup over the top of the cake and leave to cool in the pan.

*Recipe continues overleaf*

## FOR THE CANDIED ORANGES

1 cup superfine sugar

2 to 3 (blood) oranges, thinly sliced, end slices discarded

When making the candied oranges, bear in mind that blood oranges are only available seasonally, so if you can't get them, make sure you only use oranges with thinner skins and a thin layer of pith, as you will be eating all of it and, even when candied, thick orange rind can be very chewy and tart. Thinner slices of oranges and thinner layers of pith are also much easier to cut when on top of the cake. As the amount of pith can vary a lot between oranges and it's impossible to tell before slicing, I generally choose 3 to 4 oranges and use the slices with the least amount of pith and the juice from the extra 1 or 2.

Place 1 cup of water and the sugar in a large, heavy-based pan with a lid. Arrange the orange slices in a single layer in the pan and bring the mixture to a boil. Once it is boiling and the sugar has fully dissolved, cover loosely with the lid, reduce the heat to medium-low and simmer for 1 hour, or until the pith of the oranges becomes translucent and soft. Leave the oranges to cool in the pan, until they reach room temperature. Candied blood oranges can be made ahead and stored in their syrup in the refrigerator until ready to serve, then warmed to room temperature.

To serve, remove the cooled cake from the pan, peeling the parchment from the bottom. It's easier to place the cake on a cake plate or cake stand to decorate it. Gently arrange the candied blood orange slices on top of the cake. Work from the center outwards and then layer the rest of the orange slices in overlapping concentric circles. Once the cake is covered with the orange slices, spoon any remaining syrup on top to give a glossy finish, allowing a bit to drizzle down the sides.

# SAFFRON LEMON POUND CAKE

## WITH CITRUS GLAZE

This is one of my classic go-to cake recipes. In the UK, it's called a sponge cake, but in the US it's called a pound cake, as the recipe traditionally demands the same quantity (i.e. one pound) of flour, butter, and sugar.

I put yogurt in my cake batter to give it more moisture. If you prefer, you can remove the distinct flavors from this recipe—things like the saffron, cardamom, and lemon—and have a good basic cake batter recipe that you can adapt to suit your needs and flavor requirements.

## SERVES 8 TO 10

**FOR THE BATTER**
pinch of saffron
1 cup granulated sugar
2 tablespoons vodka
⅓ cup sweet rice flour
⅓ cup cornstarch
1 cup white rice flour
¼ cup ground almonds
1½ teaspoons gluten-free baking powder
½ teaspoon xanthan gum
½ teaspoon sea salt
1½ sticks unsalted butter, room temperature
2 free-range eggs
1 teaspoon ground cardamom
grated zest of 3 lemons
1 teaspoon vanilla extract
1 cup plain or coconut yogurt

**FOR THE SYRUP**
¼ cup lemon juice
¼ cup granulated or superfine sugar

**FOR THE GLAZE**
1 cup confectioner's sugar
3 to 4 tablespoons lemon juice
a handful of sliced almonds

Preheat the oven to 350°F and grease and line a loaf pan (about 8.5 x 4.5 inches) with parchment paper.

Stir the saffron with a teaspoon of the sugar in a small bowl. Add the vodka and cover with plastic wrap for 1 hour, until the saffron is fully infused. In a bowl, sift the flours, ground almonds, baking powder, xanthan gum, and salt.

Cream the butter and remaining sugar together in an electric mixer with the paddle attachment for about 5 minutes, until light and fluffy. With the mixer on low, add the eggs, one at a time, until incorporated. Add the saffron and vodka mixture, cardamom, lemon zest, and vanilla and mix until combined. Add a third of the dry ingredients with the mixer still on low and, when barely incorporated, add half the yogurt. Continue to alternate, adding the next third of the dry ingredients, followed by the remaining half of the yogurt, finishing with the final third of dry ingredients. Scrape down the sides of the bowl as you go.

When the batter has come together, turn off the mixer and scrape into the prepared pan. Smooth the top and place in the oven. Bake for 40 to 50 minutes, or until a skewer inserted into the center comes out clean. Remove from the oven and leave to cool in the pan.

To make the syrup, place the lemon juice and sugar in a saucepan. Cook over a low heat for 5 minutes, stirring to dissolve the sugar. With the cooled cake still in the pan, poke holes in the top with a skewer. Brush the cake with the syrup, until it has all been absorbed. Cool in the pan, then remove with the aid of the parchment paper.

To make the glaze, sift the confectioner's sugar into a bowl and add the lemon juice. Whisk until smooth. Pour over the top of the cooled cake and allow to drizzle down the sides. Before the glaze has hardened, sprinkle a line of flaked almonds down the center.

# BRILLIANT BANANA BREAD

I have been making this recipe for so long and it never gets boring. There is something almost medicinal about a good slice of warm banana bread and a mug of coffee. You can bake and store it for a few days although, to be honest, in my house it doesn't usually last more than a few hours!

## SERVES 8

1 cup gluten-free all-purpose flour

½ cup sorghum flour

1 teaspoon gluten-free baking powder

1 teaspoon baking soda

pinch of sea salt

1 teaspoon ground cinnamon (optional)

1 stick unsalted butter, roughly chopped and softened

1 cup superfine sugar

2 free-range eggs, lightly beaten

3 very ripe bananas, mashed with a fork, plus 1 for decoration

⅓ cup plus 2 tablespoons buttermilk (or regular milk with a squeeze of lemon juice)

¾ cup walnuts

confectioner's sugar, for dusting

Preheat the oven to 350°F.

Grease a loaf pan (about 8.5 x 4.5 inches) and line the base and sides with parchment paper.

Place all the ingredients (except the walnuts and the extra banana) in a food processor and pulse until just smooth. Be careful not to over-process.

Transfer the mixture to a bowl and stir through the walnuts. Spoon into the prepared pan and smooth the top. Slice the remaining banana and use to decorate the top.

Bake for about 55 to 60 minutes, or until the top is firm and golden brown. A skewer inserted into the center should come out clean.

Leave to cool in the pan for 10 minutes before turning out onto a wire rack to cool completely. Serve dusted with confectioner's sugar.

# SWEET PIE CRUST

Making my favorite sweet pastry gluten free was a little tricky. But then again, pastry in general can be a bit intimidating. Getting the right consistency and thickness, rolling it out evenly without it falling apart can take some practice. I've certainly made many tarts and pies that had to be patched together—gluten free or not.

One of the absolute musts of gluten-free pastry is that all ingredients have to be ice cold. I stick my butter in the freezer for 15 to 20 minutes before making the dough, as it makes it much easier to work with and also leads to more air bubbles forming when the fats expand during baking, which is where all the flakiness comes from.

This pie crust is definitely more delicate than a standard crust, as it doesn't have the gluten binding it together, so you have to be gentle and take care when rolling it out. Any gluten-free dough will also be stickier, so I advise rolling your dough on a piece of floured parchment paper. To make life easier, you can prepare this recipe and then freeze the dough for up to two to three months.

This pastry will work perfectly for my Nana's Apple Pie recipe (see page 146), but you can use any fruits such as blackberries to make a fabulous and fruity pie, or indeed any kind of sweet tart with this crust.

## MAKES 2 SHEETS

½ cup millet flour
¾ cup gluten-free oat flour
1 cup sweet rice flour
½ cup cornstarch
¼ cup tapioca starch
2 teaspoons superfine sugar
1 teaspoon xanthan gum
½ teaspoon sea salt
2 sticks unsalted butter
6 tablespoons buttermilk (or regular milk with 1 teaspoon apple cider vinegar)
6 to 8 tablespoons iced water

Sift together the flours. Mix all the dry ingredients in a bowl and work in the cold butter to make a crumble (you can use your fingers or pulse in a food processor).

Knead until a dough forms—this should take about 5 minutes. Place the dough onto a sheet of plastic wrap, flatten into a disc, and chill in the refrigerator for 30 minutes. If you are freezing the dough, wrap in a new piece of plastic wrap or place in a freezer bag.

Roll out as required on a piece of floured parchment paper.

# NANA AND THE EASY APPLE PIE

I always loved to watch my grandmother in the kitchen. There was an ease of movement and an air of complete comfort that I had never seen before. With my mom, there was always a hint of awkwardness—pans clattered, things got burned, and new recipes seemed more like failed experiments than special treats. Even my own fledgling forays in baking and cooking, which I loved, and which gave me such a sense of satisfaction, were also accompanied by a trail of dirty dishes and an undercurrent of stress. I was always afraid that something would go wrong.

But Nana made everything seem effortless—something I now recognize, in its way, as the highest level of skill and one to which I still aspire. All the things I learned in culinary school—clean as you go, don't waste food, move quickly, keep a small and tidy workspace—came naturally to her.

When Nana cooked for us, she, unlike my parents, didn't particularly care what we had for dinner, or whether we finished our meals and ate all our veggies. Whether we ate what she made, or wanted breakfast for dinner and dessert on top of that, she was completely unfazed. As long as no one complained or went to bed hungry, we could eat what we liked. This sort of culinary freedom and indulgence—coupled with Nana's great food—was exhilarating for us, as children.

I'll always remember one time, when I was about 13 or 14, and Nana was looking after us in Connecticut. It was just an ordinary week, but one day, after school, Nana decided to make apple pie. It was autumn, we had lots of apples, so why not? It may sound simple, but this sort of impromptu pie making was unprecedented in my family. My mom, and sometimes even my dad, would make homemade apple pies, but only a couple times a year for Thanksgiving or Christmas. And the infrequent making of these pies was always fraught with difficulty and disaster. Like the time my dad forgot the sugar, rendering the pie inedible. Or the time the foil covering the outside edge of the crust fell onto the bottom of the oven, caught fire, and infused the entire pie (and kitchen) with putrid smoke. Or the time a perfect, beautifully baked pie was dropped on the floor when being taken out of the oven. So apple pie was a serious and risky dessert, only for special occasions—and definitely not the sort of dish you spontaneously decide to make on a Wednesday afternoon.

Yet watching Nana make that pie made it seem like the simplest thing in the world. No trip to the supermarket, no fuss, and virtually no equipment needed. Rather than sullying a peeler, bowl, cutting board, and whatever other equipment I had thought necessary, Nana simply used a paring knife, both for peeling the apples and then deftly cutting them into thin slices straight into the pie crust. I remember being in awe of the simplicity of it and of how adroitly her fingers moved with the knife and each apple. I asked her how she managed to peel and slice like that and she answered, "Well, I've had 40 years of practice. Someday, it will be just as easy for you." And those words have always stuck with me—because cooking really is largely a matter of practice and trial and error. The more you do it, the better you get.

To this day, apple pie is one of my favorite desserts to make for my family and for the holidays. And even those times when the crust breaks and doesn't come out perfectly, I still feel a sense of calm as I patch it up because it doesn't matter—after all, it's just apple pie.

# NANA'S APPLE PIE

There is nothing more American than apple pie, or so the saying goes. However, I learned how to make my perfect apple pie from my Scottish grandmother, so go figure! (For the full story, see page 145.)

Apple pie became one of my signature dishes when I was just 12, spending a lot of time off school with Lyme disease and discovering my love of cooking.

Each element here is so important. The crust has to be buttery, yet flaky. I know it seems like a lot of work for such a simple dish, but trust me—the perfectly browned pie, with its flaky layers and caramel glaze of juices on the side, bubbling up as you remove it from the oven, makes it all worthwhile.

## SERVES 8

### FOR THE PIE CRUST
1 quantity Sweet Pie Crust (see page 144), or 1½ pounds gluten-free store-bought puff pastry (as gluten-free pie crust is hard to find in stores)

### FOR THE FILLING
1 pound Golden Delicious apples, peeled, cored, and thinly sliced

1 pound Granny Smith apples, peeled, cored, and thinly sliced

⅓ cup superfine sugar

½ teaspoon ground cinnamon

1 tablespoon lemon juice

½ teaspoon vanilla extract

2 tablespoons cornstarch

### TO FINISH
1 to 2 tablespoons milk

1 tablespoon granulated sugar

Preheat the oven to 400°F.

Divide the pastry into two pieces—one slightly larger than the other to cover the top of pie.

Place the smaller section of dough onto a piece of parchment paper and roll out into a 12-inch circle. Ease the dough into a 9-inch pie dish and trim off any overhang. This dough has a tendency to crack when placing it in the dish, but simply press any cracks or fissures together with your hands to repair them and it will all bake together just fine. Chill in the refrigerator while you prepare the filling.

Place the apples in a large bowl. Mix with the sugar, cinnamon, lemon juice, and vanilla extract. Leave to marinate for 5 minutes, until juices start to form. Add the cornstarch to thicken the apple juices, then transfer the mixture into the chilled pastry base.

Roll the second piece of pastry onto a piece of parchment paper into a 12 to 13-inch circle. Carefully lift the pastry onto the pie to cover the fruit filling. Trim the excess dough from the top and sides. To crimp the edges of the crust, use one finger to push the pastry down on the outside edge of the dish. Then, pinch around that finger using a finger and thumb from your other hand, creating a scalloped effect. Cut slits into the top, brush with the milk and sprinkle with granulated sugar.

Bake for 15 minutes, then reduce temperature to 350°F for a further 45 to 50 minutes, until the crust is golden brown.

# PLUM CROSTATA

Somewhere between the pie, the galette, and the tart lies the crostata. I love it for all its gooey fruitiness and crisp pastry case and the best thing is that unlike a more traditional French patisserie, this Italian dessert doesn't need to be too tidy and precise—which is all part of the fun.

## SERVES 6

### FOR THE DOUGH

½ cup sweet rice flour/ glutinous rice flour

¼ cup cornstarch or corn flour

¼ cup millet flour

¼ cup oat flour

¼ teaspoon coarse sea salt

½ teaspoon xanthan gum

1 teaspoon superfine sugar

6 tablespoons cold unsalted butter, cut into small pieces

3 to 4 tablespoons iced water

### FOR THE FILLING

1 pound plums, stoned and cut into eighths

6 tablespoons light brown muscovado sugar (or a combination of coconut and brown sugar)

2 tablespoons cornstarch or cornflour

¼ teaspoon ground cinnamon

finely grated zest of 1 large orange

1 tablespoon orange juice

### TO FINISH

1 tablespoon milk

1 tablespoon demerara sugar

Preheat the oven to 400°F.

To make the dough, combine the dry ingredients in a large bowl. Add the butter and rub in by hand until you have a sandy consistency. Add in the iced water slowly, as you may not need it all, and mix by hand until it comes together to form a soft dough.

Flatten the ball of dough, cover with plastic wrap and let chill in the refrigerator for 30 minutes.

Roll out the dough on a piece of parchment paper to a 10-inch circle.

Using a sharp knife, cut the edges to ensure a clean edge and then lift up the dough with the parchment paper and transfer to a baking sheet.

Mix the plums with the rest of the ingredients and leave to stand for a few minutes.

To assemble, arrange the plums in concentric circles in the center of the dough, leaving a 1-inch border around it. Gently fold the border in on top of the fruit.

To finish, brush the pastry with milk and sprinkle with demerara sugar. Bake for 40 to 50 minutes, until the filling is bubbly and the crust is brown. Leave to cool for about 30 minutes and then serve.

# CHERRY CLAFOUTIS

This is a fantastic summer dessert. There's something really rather old school and sophisticated about it, and it always makes me feel very ladylike!

You can adapt it by changing the fruit to apricots or pears, and once you have made it, it will become one of your default desserts, I promise you.

## SERVES 6 TO 8

3 cups fresh or frozen cherries, pits removed

2 tablespoons kirsch if using cherries (or apricot or pear brandy, if using apricots or pears)

1 tablespoon unsalted butter, melted, for greasing

⅓ cup granulated sugar, plus extra for the pan

4 large free-range eggs

1 teaspoon vanilla extract

¼ cup sorghum flour

2 tablespoons ground almonds

2 tablespoons coconut flour

1¼ cups almond or dairy milk

pinch of sea salt

---

Preheat the oven to 350°F.

Steep the fruit in the alcohol for at least an hour.

Grease a 9-inch round baking dish, about 1½-inch deep, with butter and sprinkle with a tablespoon of sugar. Shake off any excess.

In a bowl, whisk the eggs, sugar, and vanilla.

Sift the flours into a separate bowl and mix, then slowly add to the wet mixture. Slowly add the milk and salt, then add the fruit.

Tip the mixture into the prepared baking dish. Bake for about 35 minutes until puffy and golden. Serve immediately.

## TIP

*A clafoutis makes the perfect blank canvas for a variety of fruit—try replacing the cherries with chopped or sliced peaches, apricots, mango, or bananas.*

# PEACH, ALMOND, AND RASPBERRY CRISP

I have witnessed on countless occasions how the British somehow manage to pack in a dessert right after chowing down on a huge Sunday roast! So I thought I would offer my own Sunday lunch suggestions, as I am now living over in the UK. You really should eat this pudding (that's what Brits call any dessert—I love that word!) sitting around a big kitchen table, surrounded by friends, and possibly with a glass of red wine on the go.

A bit like any crumble, this fruity, oaty dessert comes into its own in the winter. I usually serve it with crème anglaise or custard.

## SERVES 6 TO 8

- ½ cup coconut oil, softened or melted, plus extra for greasing
- 10 ripe peaches
- 1 tablespoon cornstarch
- 1 teaspoon vanilla extract
- 1 pint raspberries, or a mixture including raspberries and blackberries
- ¾ cup light brown sugar
- ½ cup sorghum flour
- ½ cup oat flour
- ½ cup gluten-free quick cooking oats
- ½ teaspoon sea salt
- ½ teaspoon ground cinnamon
- ½ cup sliced almonds

Preheat the oven to 375°F.

Lightly grease a ceramic ovenproof dish (about 9 x 6 x 2½ inches) with coconut oil.

Place the peaches in a large heatproof bowl and cover with boiling water (from the kettle). Leave the peaches to stand for a few minutes, then drain and peel them. Remove the stones and cut the flesh into large pieces. Add the cornstarch and vanilla extract and gently stir in the raspberries. Leave to stand for 5 minutes. If there is a lot of liquid, add an extra tablespoon of cornstarch.

In a separate bowl, combine the brown sugar, sorghum flour, oat flour, oats, sea salt, and cinnamon. Add the coconut oil and mix until the topping is crumbly. Gently stir in the flaked almonds.

Pour the peach and raspberry mixture into the prepared dish. Sprinkle the topping evenly over the fruit to cover. Cook for 40 to 50 minutes.

Serve warm (or at room temperature).

# DELICIOUS HOT CHOCOLATE SOUFFLÉ

## WITH DARK CHOCOLATE SAUCE

Hands down, chocolate is the one thing I could not exist without. One or two squares of very dark chocolate is also very good for you. An antioxidant and anti-inflammatory and … well, that's all you need to know, really. So this is not a guilty dessert treat; it actually does you good.

### SERVES 8

#### FOR THE SAUCE
½ cup light cream

1 ounce superfine sugar

1 ounce unsalted butter, plus extra for greasing

4 ounces good-quality gluten-free dark chocolate, 85% cocoa solids

#### FOR THE SOUFFLÉ
4 ounces superfine sugar, plus 2 tablespoons

6 tablespoons milk

8 ounces good-quality gluten-free dark chocolate, 85% cocoa solids

4 large free-range eggs, separated, plus 2 egg whites

1 tablespoon confectioner's sugar, for dusting

Preheat the oven to 375°F.

To make the sauce, place the cream and sugar in a saucepan over a low heat, then add the butter and chocolate and melt, stirring constantly. Set aside and keep warm.

Brush eight 5-ounce ramekins with melted butter, then dust with superfine sugar and shake off any excess.

In a saucepan, warm the milk over medium-low heat. Take off the heat and add the chocolate, stirring until melted. Transfer to a bowl and leave to cool for at least 5 minutes.

In a separate bowl, beat the 4 ounces sugar and egg yolks until the mixture becomes a lighter color (about 3 minutes with an electric hand mixer), then add to the melted chocolate and milk mixture.

In a separate bowl, whisk the egg whites with a clean whisk, along with the extra 2 tablespoons sugar, until stiff peaks form.

Gently fold a third of the egg whites into the chocolate mixture with a metal spoon. Do not over-mix. Continue adding the egg whites, one third at a time until it is all used.

Transfer the mixture to the ramekins, place them on a baking sheet and bake for 25 minutes, or until the tops have risen. (Be careful to leave enough room in the oven for them to rise.)

With a skewer, quickly make a small hole in the top of each soufflé and pour in the warm chocolate sauce (if you find it has cooled and thickened too much, simply warm over a low heat). You can also use a disposable zip-top bag with a corner snipped off for this.

Dust with confectioner's sugar and serve quickly!

# MOCHA AND CREAM DACQUOISE

## SERVES 8 TO 10

### FOR THE DACQUOISE

2 cups blanched hazelnuts

1½ cups superfine sugar

¼ cup cornstarch

6 large free-range egg whites

pinch of sea salt

confectioner's sugar, for dusting

### FOR THE MOCHA FILLING

⅔ cup superfine sugar

2 tablespoons instant coffee dissolved in ¼ cup boiling water

¼ cup cornstarch

1 cup milk

2 cups whipping cream

3 free-range egg yolks

2 ounces good-quality gluten-free dark chocolate

2 tablespoons butter

### FOR THE CHANTILLY CREAM FILLING

1 cup heavy cream

¼ cup confectioner's sugar

½ tablespoon Frangelico liqueur (or dark rum)

### FOR THE PRALINE HAZELNUTS

¼ cup superfine sugar

30 whole blanched hazelnuts

### FOR THE DECORATION

¼ cup chopped, toasted hazelnuts

Dacquoise, despite its elaborate French name, is easy to put together once the individual components are made—it's basically a fancy version of an icebox cake and is naturally gluten free. The trickiest part is making the meringues, but don't worry about them being perfect—the bottom two layers merge with the fillings and any imperfections on the top can be hidden beneath a snowy dusting of confectioner's sugar. The whole cake needs about 12 hours in the refrigerator, once assembled, for the meringue and the fillings to truly blend together—it's a long process, but definitely worth the wait.

---

Preheat the oven to 350°F.

Begin with the dacquoise. Place the hazelnuts in a food processor and pulse until coarsely ground. Spread the nuts on a baking sheet and bake for 10 to 12 minutes or until golden brown. Remove from the oven and transfer to a bowl to cool. Add ½ cup of the superfine sugar and the cornstarch.

Reduce the oven temperature to 300°F.

Mark circles on three pieces of parchment paper, approximately 8 inches in diameter. Line three baking sheets with the paper circles.

To make the meringue, beat the egg whites in an electric mixer, using the whisk attachment. Add the salt and whisk on medium speed until frothy. Add the remaining superfine sugar a third at a time, making sure each addition is fully incorporated before adding more. The meringue should form stiff peaks. Use a spoon to gently fold the ground hazelnut mixture through the meringue.

Spoon the meringue mixture into a large piping bag with a plain ½-inch nozzle and pipe onto the first paper circle in a spiral, starting at the center and working outwards to fill it. Dust with confectioner's sugar, then repeat with the other two circles. Bake for 1 hour, making sure they don't catch and start to burn—you may want to swap over the top and bottom trays in the oven to ensure an even bake. Turn off the oven after an hour and open the door, but leave the meringue to cool in the oven, for at least 30 to 35 minutes minutes. (If you have any meringue mixture left over, then why not bake some little meringue swirls and use for a pavlova with fruit and cream?)

*Recipe continues overleaf*

To make the mocha filling, melt together the sugar, instant coffee, and cornstarch in a saucepan over a low heat, then set aside.

In a bowl, whisk the milk, half the cream and egg yolks. Slowly add the egg mixture to the sugar and coffee mixture, whisking to avoid any lumps. Transfer to a saucepan and bring the mixture to a boil over a medium heat, whisking for 1 to 2 minutes to avoid any lumps forming, until the mixture has thickened and coats the back of a spoon. Remove from heat. In a bain-marie (a small bowl set over a saucepan of simmering water), melt the chocolate and butter. (You can also do this in a microwave for about 1 minute.)

Add the chocolate and butter mix to the custard and leave to cool at room temperature for an hour.

In a separate bowl, whisk the other half of the cream into peaks and then fold into the cooled custard to make it spreadable. Chill in the refrigerator for 30 to 40 minutes to firm up a little.

To make the Chantilly cream filling, whip the cream, confectioner's sugar, and Frangelico in an electric mixer or with an electric hand mixer until stiff peaks form. Set aside.

Finally, prepare the hazelnut praline: line a baking sheet with parchment paper. Place the sugar in a small, heavy-bottomed saucepan and gently heat until it turns golden-brown or reaches 356°F. Add the hazelnuts, a few at a time, and coat in the caramel, then remove with a spoon and place the coated hazelnuts individually on the lined sheet. You will have to work quickly to cover all 30 hazelnuts as the caramel will begin to set. Leave to cool.

To assemble the dacquoise, place one of the meringue layers on a large, flat serving plate and spread with half the mocha filling. Place another meringue layer on top and spread with the remaining mocha filling. Then place the final meringue layer on top.

Using an offset spatula, spread the Chantilly cream around the sides of the assembled dacquoise and then sprinkle the toasted chopped hazelnuts on top of the cream to decorate the sides. Save a little of the cream to stick the hazelnut pralines to the top meringue layer.

Dust the top with confectioner's sugar and decorate the edges of the meringue with praline hazelnuts, using a little spot of cream to stick them on.

Refrigerate the finished dacquoise overnight before serving.

# LEMON AND LIMONCELLO SORBET

This dessert transports me to the Amalfi coast of Italy, where lemons literally drip off the trees and into limoncello—the stickiest and most delectable liqueur. Everyone makes their own version over there. If you can eat this sitting in Positano overlooking the sea, then I would thoroughly recommend it.

## SERVES 8 TO 10

8 to 10 lemons
1½ cups superfine sugar
juice of 2 to 3 lemons (about ½ cup)
grated zest of 2 lemons, grated
½ cup limoncello
pinch of sea salt

### TO SERVE
⅔ cup Prosecco (optional)

With a sharp knife, cut a slice of around ¾-inch from the top of each lemon to open it up. Using a teaspoon, carve out the pulp and seeds. (You can press the pulp through a seive for the lemon juice and use it in this recipe or maybe keep it for cocktails!)

Cut a strip off the bottom off each lemon, so it can stand upright, but not so deep that you put a hole in the bottom. Pop the lemons on parchment paper on a baking sheet and freeze.

In a saucepan, bring 2 cups of water and the sugar to a boil and stir into a syrup. Remove from the heat and leave to cool. Transfer the syrup to a freezer-proof bowl and add the lemon juice, zest, limoncello, and salt, and stir well. Freeze for at least 2 hours.

Transfer to an ice-cream maker and follow the manufacturer's instructions. Then freeze again for at least 2 hours. (You can keep the dish in the freezer overnight, stirring occasionally, if you don't have an ice-cream maker.)

For a truly authentic Italian touch, take half the frozen sorbet and soften at room temperature for 10 minutes. Then place in a bowl and whisk by hand until soft and creamy and add ½ cup Prosecco, a little at a time, whisking until fully incorporated. Pour a little of the Prosecco sorbet into the bottom of each of the frozen lemons. Then top with the regular sorbet and serve.

# MASCARPONE CHEESECAKE

## WITH ROASTED GRAPES

This amazingly addictive cheesecake needs to be chilled well before serving, so if you can, make it the day before you want to serve it. I use amaretti cookies for this recipe, but make sure you get ones that are gluten free, as not all are. The base can also be made with a plain sweet gluten-free cookie. To make the filling easier to combine, remove the cream cheese and mascarpone from the refrigerator about an hour before starting.

## SERVES 8 TO 10

### FOR THE CHEESECAKE

3½ ounces crisp gluten-free amaretti cookies

⅓ cup ground almonds

2 knobs ginger in syrup, drained

½ stick butter, melted

16 ounces cream cheese, at room temperature

8 ounces mascarpone

1 cup superfine sugar

1 to 2 tablespoons cornstarch

4 free-range eggs

2 teaspoons vanilla extract

finely grated zest of 1 lemon

### FOR THE FROSTED GRAPES

bunch of black grapes, on the vine

1 tablespoon olive oil

superfine sugar, for sprinkling

Preheat the oven to 375°F.

Grease a 9-inch springform pan and line the base with parchment paper.

Place the cookies, almonds, ginger, and melted butter in a food processor and pulse until the mixture comes together. Press into the base of the prepared pan and chill in the refrigerator for 30 minutes. Bake for 12 minutes, then remove and leave to cool.

Cover the outside of the pan (base and sides) with 2 layers of foil. It must be watertight.

Place the cream cheese, mascarpone, sugar, and cornstarch in an electric stand mixer and beat until creamy and well combined. Add the eggs, one at a time, then beat in the vanilla and lemon zest. Beat for 2 to 3 minutes or until the mixture is light and fluffy. Spoon onto the base and smooth the top. Cover with foil.

Place the foil-wrapped pan in a large roasting tin and fill it with enough boiling water to come halfway up the sides. Bake for 65 to 70 minutes, or until just set in middle. Turn off the oven and leave the cheesecake to cool in the oven for 30 minutes before removing.

Leave to cool and then refrigerate for at least 6 hours.

An hour before serving preheat the oven to 425°F. Place the entire bunch of grapes in a baking dish. Drizzle with the olive oil, sprinkle with sugar, and bake for 5 to 10 minutes, until golden. Remove from the oven and leave to cool for 20 minutes.

Release the cheesecake from the pan and transfer to a serving plate. Decorate with the grapes, removing a few to scatter alongside.

# MUST-HAVE MATCHA CHOCOLATE MOUSSE

Two of my favorite things in the world—matcha tea and chocolate—in one dish. Heaven!

## SERVES 4

1 teaspoon matcha powder (the best quality you can find—I like Lalani & Co)

1 cup heavy cream

4 ounces gluten-free white chocolate

1 vanilla pod

Place a heatproof bowl over a pan of boiling water. Sift in the matcha powder and then slowly whisk in (with a traditional matcha whisk, if you have one) half the cream. Add the chocolate and melt, whisking to avoid any lumps.

Remove from the heat and leave to cool.

Halve the vanilla pod lengthways and scrape the seeds into the chocolate mixture. Add the remaining cream and whisk with an electric hand mixer for 2 to 3 minutes, until the mousse is just holding its shape—take care not to over-whisk.

Divide the mixture between four 4-ounce ramekins or glasses. Chill in the refrigerator for at least an hour before serving.

## INGREDIENT NOTE

*A Japanese staple, matcha has been the hot trend for the past year or two and gives a real sense of calm. Usually taken as a tea, the powder can also be used in cooking. There are different qualities and varieties for this. It has a fantastic bright green color, which works not only for desserts and ice creams, but also for matcha lattes and sweets.*

# EXOTIC ROSE AND CARDAMOM MILK PUDDING

## SERVES 6

1 cup superfine sugar

4 tablespoons ground rice

4 tablespoons cornstarch

4 cups milk

4 cardamom pods, lightly crushed

large handful (about 2 ounces) pistachios, roasted and crushed, to serve

1 tablespoon rosewater

a handful of edible rose petals, to serve

Rose flavor in any pudding is one of those things that makes me go all Arabian Nights … when you combine the rose with cardamom and pistachios you are instantly transported to somewhere truly exotic. The creamy texture of the milk creates a luxurious backdrop for these intense flavors that feel a little bit Indian and a little Middle Eastern, all in one delightful dish.

Preheat the oven to 325°F.

Place the sugar, ground rice, and cornstarch in a blender. Slowly add the milk and blend until smooth.

Transfer the mixture to a saucepan, set over a medium heat and add the crushed (but still intact) cardamom pods. Bring to the boil, stirring constantly. Reduce the heat and simmer for 5 to 10 minutes, until thickened, stirring throughout. Remove from the heat and leave to cool.

Meanwhile, line a baking sheet with parchment paper. Spread out the pistachios on the tray and bake for 6 to 8 minutes.

Remove the cardamom pods from the saucepan, add half the roasted pistachios and the rosewater and mix. Spoon into small bowls (5 to 7 oz.) and chill in the refrigerator for at least 2 hours.

To serve, sprinkle with the remaining roasted pistachios and rose petals.

## TIP

*Make sure the roses that you use are from unsprayed specimens; trim off the little white base of the petal as these may be bitter.*

# PACIUGO

## WITH DARK CHOCOLATE ICE CREAM

I first had this in the Hotel Splendido in Portofino—and a more delicious and fabulously Italian dessert you could not wish to taste. You do need an ice-cream maker to achieve the desired smoothness, but it's well worth it. This is summer captured in a dish. The only problem is you will always want more. *Bellissima!*

### SERVES 6

#### FOR THE CHOCOLATE ICE CREAM

2 cups heavy cream

3 tablespoons raw cocoa powder

5 ounces good-quality gluten-free dark chocolate, 70% cocoa solids, chopped

5 large free-range egg yolks

½ teaspoon vanilla extract

1 cup whole milk

¾ cup granulated sugar

pinch of sea salt

#### FOR THE PACIUGO

4 ounces morello cherries in syrup, plus extra to serve

4 ounces pineapple pieces, chopped

4 ounces blueberries

¾ cup plus 2 tablespoons heavy cream

To make the ice cream, gently warm 1 cup of the cream with the cocoa powder in a heavy-based saucepan over a low heat, whisking continuously. Bring to the boil and remove from the heat. Add the chocolate and stir until smooth. Add the remaining cream and continue to mix. Transfer to a bowl.

In a separate bowl, whisk the egg yolks and vanilla, so the eggs are creamy and turning pale.

In another saucepan, warm the milk, sugar, and salt. Pour the warm milk mixture onto the egg yolks. Make sure the milk is not too hot and whisk constantly to avoid scrambling the eggs. Once mixed, return the yolk and milk mixture back to the saucepan and reheat, stirring constantly.

Pour the warm yolk and milk mixture over the chocolate mixture and keep whisking until smooth. Pour the mixture into a container and refrigerate for at least 1 hour. Transfer to an ice-cream maker and continue according to the manufacturer's instructions.

When you're ready to make the paciugo, remove the chocolate gelato from the freezer for a little while to soften. Line six 1-cup sundae glasses with morello cherry syrup. Sprinkle with the pineapple pieces, blueberries, and cherries.

Cover with softened dark chocolate gelato and scrape the top to leave a flat surface. Place in the freezer.

Whip the cream to medium-soft peaks. Take the glasses out of the freezer and cover the gelato layer with whipped cream. Drizzle with morello syrup and top each glass with 2 to 3 cherries to serve.

# UNICORN MARSH-MALLOWS

OK, so not exactly made from unicorns… but when you see the super cool pastel colors and the amazing food science at work in this recipe, you will see just how much wonderment and joy one tiny sweet thing can cause. I have to say, if only my chemistry lessons at school had been like this, then who knows what might have happened? For anyone a little nervous of using food coloring, there are some really great natural food colors for sale now, or you can also use natural freeze-dried foods—I have used blueberry and raspberry in the past. I guarantee the sight of the marshmallow mixture expanding and taking on the colors will get any kids you know into the kitchen and interested in the possibilities of food and cooking.

## MAKES ABOUT 32

oil, for greasing

1½ cups coconut water

3 tablespoons powdered gelatin

¼ teaspoon cream of tartar

¼ teaspoon sea salt

2 cups granulated sugar

¼ cup honey

1 teaspoon vanilla extract

1 teaspoon coconut extract

1 to 2 drops natural pink food coloring

1 to 2 drops natural green food coloring

1 to 2 drops natural blue food coloring

1 to 2 drops natural purple food coloring

1 to 2 drops natural yellow food coloring

2 tablespoons cornstarch, for dusting

2 tablespoons confectioner's sugar, for dusting

Oil an 8 x 8 inch pan and line with parchment paper. Lightly oil the paper.

Pour ½ cup coconut water into a large stand mixer bowl, sprinkle the gelatin on the top and leave to soften. Add the cream of tartar and salt and beat on high speed for 2 to 3 minutes, until fluffy.

Place the remaining coconut water in a saucepan with the sugar and honey and cook on a medium-low heat until the sugar has dissolved. Keep stirring and increase the temperature. Check with a thermometer—the mixture needs to reach 240°F.

Carefully, pour the cooled syrup mixture into the gelatin mixture still in the mixer bowl. Add the vanilla and coconut extracts and beat on low speed, until combined. Increase the speed to high and continue to beat until fluffy and the mixture has tripled in volume, about 6 minutes (you want to make sure it's still a little bit warm to work with).

Meanwhile, arrange 5 separate bowls on the worktop and put a different food color in each. (If you are using the powders, mix each one with 2 teaspoons water to dissolve first, so that the color mixes evenly through the marshmallow.) Lightly oil 5 spoons or spatulas, one for each bowl.

*Recipe continues overleaf*

Spoon a fifth of the marshmallow into each one of the bowls. Mix quickly with the oiled spoon or spatula to take on the color and then scrape the marshmallow into the lined pan, spreading it across the base. Repeat, one at a time, with each of the remaining colors, layering them one on top of the other in the pan. You will need to work quickly, before the marshmallow starts to set.

Using an oiled knife, swirl through the mixture to create a marbled effect. Do not overwork it or you will lose the marble effect. Dip the knife in cold water and smooth the surface. Cover with a lightly oiled piece of parchment paper and set aside in a cool cupboard overnight to fully set.

The next day, using a lightly oiled sharp knife, tip the marshmallow out onto another sheet of parchment paper and slice into cubes.

In a small bowl, mix the cornstarch and confectioner's sugar and use to cover the sides of each cube. Serve with a mug of hot chocolate for the ultimate sleepover treat—whatever your age!

## TIP

*You can use natural freeze-dried foods as coloring—simply mix them up with a little bit of water. Some people suggest using turmeric as a yellow color and chlorophyll or spirulina as a green food coloring—they may work in some dishes, but I would absolutely avoid those in this recipe as the flavors of marshmallow are just too subtle to take these two beasts on. So use natural dyes for these colors.*

# GLUTEN-FREE BROWN BREAD

Bread is such an ancient and intrinsic part of the human experience that it feels like it is written into our DNA. Farming wheat took us from primitive hunter-gatherers to the civilised beings we supposedly are today. The baking and eating of bread is one of the most fundamental human rituals, forming the basis of ceremonies in many religions. It transcends civilisation, culture, and denomination, and thus 'breaking bread' with someone is the saying that represents our fundamental, ageless gesture of connecting with another human being.

## MAKES 1 LOAF

oil, for greasing
2 free-range egg whites
1 tablespoon molasses
3 cups gluten-free brown bread flour (see Tip)
½ cup brown rice flour
1 cup oat flour
2 teaspoons xanthan gum
1 (¼ ounce) packet dried active baking yeast
1 teaspoon sea salt
milk, for brushing

Preheat the oven to 425°F.

Grease a loaf pan (about 8.5 x 4.5 inches) with a little oil.

Place the egg whites and treacle in a measuring cup and add enough warm water to make it up to 2 cups.

Combine the flours, xanthan gum, yeast, and salt in large bowl. Make a well in the center and add the water, egg-white and treacle mixture. Using a large metal spoon, mix until combined and smooth (this will take about 3 to 4 minutes). You will have a fairly soft dough (more like a cake batter), but that is fine. Transfer to the prepared tin, cover with plastic wrap and set aside in a warm place for about 1½ hours (it will rise by about a third to a half in size).

Brush the top of the loaf with a little milk. Transfer the pan to the oven and bake for 45 to 55 minutes, or until risen and golden. Leave to cool in the pan for 10 minutes, before turning out onto a wire rack to cool completely. The bread should keep for 4 to 5 days.

## TIP

*If gluten-free brown bread flour is not available, it's best to mix your own blend. Equal quantities of brown rice flour, sorghum flour, and gluten-free cornmeal would work well.*

# CLASSIC WHITE BREAD

This is one of the first breads that I learnt to make gluten free and it's a simple recipe to get started with. I usually make more than one loaf at a time and then freeze, as gluten-free bread doesn't last very long, so it's a good idea to have another loaf ready to go. You can always make a stale loaf into breadcrumbs and freeze for later as well.

## MAKES 1 LOAF

oil, for greasing

2 free-range egg whites

2½ cups gluten-free plain flour (I use Cup4Cup)

4 ounces rice flour

⅓ cup potato flour

2 teaspoons xanthan gum

1 tablespoon granulated sugar

1 (¼ ounce) packet dried active baking yeast

1 teaspoon sea salt

milk, for brushing

Preheat the oven to 425°F.

Grease a loaf pan (about 8.5 x 4.5 inches) with a little oil.

Place the egg whites in a measuring cup and add enough warm water to make it up to 2 cups.

Combine the flours, xanthan gum, sugar, yeast, and salt in large bowl. Make a well in the center and add the water and egg-white mixture. Using a large metal spoon, mix until combined and smooth (about 3 to 4 minutes). This will be a fairly soft, dough-like batter.

Transfer to the prepared pan, cover with plastic wrap and set aside in a warm place for 1½ hours (it will rise by about a third to a half in size).

Brush the top of the loaf with a little milk and transfer the pan to the oven to bake for 45 to 55 minutes, or until risen and golden.

Leave to cool in the pan for 10 minutes before turning out onto a wire rack to cool completely.

# ZA'ATAR FLATBREAD

I have already mentioned how much I love Middle Eastern flavors. I am using spices like za'atar and sumac increasingly in my cooking; it's so exciting when you find new ideas and combinations to excite the taste buds—especially when you discover them when travelling.

The traditional way of using za'atar is like this, in a flatbread. You can eat this with olives and labneh (see page 98) or it's equally as delicious on its own.

## MAKES 8

2 cups gluten-free white bread flour (I use Cup4Cup), plus extra for dusting

1 teaspoon gluten-free baking powder

1 teaspoon xanthan gum

1 teaspoon sea salt

2 tablespoons za'atar

1 cup plain yogurt

Preheat the broiler to high and dust a baking sheet with a little gluten-free flour.

Combine the flour, baking powder, xanthan gum, salt, and half the za'atar. Stir in the yogurt and ½ cup water. Mix with a large metal spoon until combined and you have a soft dough.

Divide the dough into 8 equal pieces, then roll out and shape each one on a lightly floured surface to about ¼-inch thick.

Dust lightly with a little flour and sprinkle with a pinch of the remaining za'atar.

Transfer 2 or three 3 of the flatbreads onto the prepared baking sheet and place under the broiler. Broil for 4 to 5 minutes on each side, until golden and puffed.

Serve warm.

# FRENCH BAGUETTE

I love bread in pretty much all its forms, but my all-time favorite has got to be the classic French baguette. Hot from the oven, ripped apart with butter melting onto its soft fluffy insides—nothing can beat it. So it was just a bit heartbreaking to discover there were so few gluten-free baguette options available. I had to learn to make my own. I'll be honest, this was a recipe I struggled with for a while— the structure does not adapt easily to gluten free. So I had to throw out my traditionally trained ideas of how the dough should be made and what it should look like, as well as a lot of unsuccessful, deflated baguettes. I was so happy when I finally found a combination and method that worked. In baking any baguette, having steam in the oven is essential. Also having a perforated baguette pan is a must as it holds the dough into the right shape as it bakes and allows the steam to get through and create that delicious golden exterior.

## MAKES 2 BAGUETTES

2 tablespoons dried active baking yeast

1 cup warm water

1 tablespoon sugar

¾ cup sorghum flour

¼ cup sweet rice flour

½ cup millet flour

½ cup brown rice flour

1 cup tapioca starch

2 teaspoons xanthan gum (or guar gum)

1½ teaspoons sea salt

3 free-range egg whites (yolks reserved)

1 teaspoon white wine vinegar

2 to 3 tablespoons olive oil

2 tablespoons salted butter, melted

cornmeal, for dusting

Preheat the oven to 400°F. Brush a baguette pan (which will usually fit at least two baguettes) with olive oil and dust with cornmeal.

Mix the yeast with the water and sugar. This will make the yeast start to work. Set aside for 20 minutes in a warm place and you will see bubbles appear on the surface. Meanwhile, mix the dry ingredients together in the bowl of a stand mixer on low.

In a separate bowl, mix the egg whites, vinegar, and olive oil together. Add to the dry ingredients, mixing on low until combined. With the mixer still on low, pour in the proofed yeast mixture. Increase the speed and beat on high for 3 minutes, until the mixture is well mixed and everything is incorporated.

Be aware that the mixture will feel very wet and it will be difficult to handle. Don't worry! Divide the mixture in two and, using a spoon, place into the baguette pan. Using wet hands, shape the dough into smooth oval loaves. Slash the top diagonally three times with a sharp knife. Repeat to make the other loaf and set the baguettes near the preheated oven or in a warm environment to rise for 30 to 45 minutes, or until they have doubled in size.

Meanwhile, boil enough water to almost fill a 9-x-13-inch roasting pan. Place the pan on the lowest rack of the oven and pour the water in 10 minutes before you are ready to bake the baguettes. This creates a steamy environment for the bread to bake in, giving the loaves a good crust. Right before placing the pan in the oven, use a spray bottle to spritz some water into the oven as well.

Brush the top of the baguettes with melted butter, that has been cooled and mixed with half the reserved egg yolks. This will create a brown crust. Bake in the oven for 25 to 30 minutes, until golden and cooked through.

# CHEESE AND CHIVE SCONES

There is an age-old debate about the scone—not only how to pronounce it, but also whether the British or the US version is better. I have decided to make a savory version that is rooted in a recipe I learned from my nana. She was Scottish, so I suppose that lays my hat on the British side of the pond for this argument. I am told they are delicious when cold, but to be honest I have never managed to get these beyond the kitchen table! As the smell of them baking fills my apartment, friends suddenly appear at my door. Who needs social media? Just make cheesy scones!

## MAKES 12

2 cups gluten-free all-purpose flour, plus extra for kneading

1 teaspoon xanthan gum powder

2 teaspoons gluten-free baking powder

½ teaspoon baking soda

½ teaspoon mustard powder

pinch of sea salt

½ stick salted butter, chilled and diced, plus extra to serve

1½ cups Cheddar, grated

2 tablespoons chopped chives

1 cup milk

1 teaspoon lemon juice

Preheat the oven to 400°F.

Line a baking sheet with parchment paper.

Sift the flour, xanthan gum, baking powder, baking soda, mustard powder, and a pinch of salt into a large bowl. Add the butter and, using your fingertips, rub it into the flour until the mixture resembles fine breadcrumbs. Mix in two thirds of the Cheddar and the chives.

Whisk together the milk and lemon juice (it will curdle, but don't panic) and pour most of the milk into the flour mixture (reserving 1 to 2 tablespoons).

Mix gently, with a large metal spoon, until it just comes together to form a wet dough—but be careful not to overwork it. Gather into a rough ball shape, then turn out onto a lightly floured surface and knead very lightly. The dough should feel slightly wet.

Gently flatten out the dough to a thickness of 1¼ inch and cut into 12 medium or 15 small squares. Gently shape into rounds and transfer to the prepared baking sheet, ½ inch apart. Brush the tops with the remaining milk and sprinkle with the remaining Cheddar. Bake for 15 to 20 minutes, or until golden and risen.

Serve warm with butter and prepare to melt!

# FOCACCIA
## WITH HEIRLOOM TOMATOES

I struck gold when I tried to make focaccia, gluten-free. I'll never forget the simultaneous feeling of shock and bliss I felt as I took that first warm bite. Finally, I had recreated a bread without gluten that worked: a real focaccia with its perfect, springy texture and infused with the flavors of olive oil, rosemary, and garlic. It was just like the focaccia of my memory and so I ate the whole loaf by myself and promptly made another one.

This recipe was so important to me in my evolution as a gluten-free cook. It gave me the confidence to create many more and the hope that I wouldn't have to live the rest of my life without this most basic and delicious of foods—because, for me, a life without bread is a life not worth living.

## MAKES 2 LOAVES

2 cups sorghum flour

2 cups potato starch or tapioca starch (do not mistake potato starch for potato flour)

1 cup millet flour

4 teaspoons xanthan gum

2½ teaspoons sea salt, plus extra for sprinkling

2 garlic cloves, minced

2 teaspoons each chopped rosemary, thyme, and basil, plus extra for sprinkling

2 tablespoons dried active baking yeast

pinch of sugar

2½ to 2⅔ cups warm water (at 110°F)

½ cup extra virgin olive oil, plus extra for drizzling

2 tablespoons honey

1 teaspoon rice vinegar (or lemon juice)

2 free-range eggs, beaten

2 large heirloom tomatoes, thinly sliced

gluten-free cornmeal, for dusting

Dust two baking sheets with cornmeal.

Mix the flours, xanthan gum, salt, garlic, and herbs together.

Stir the yeast with the sugar into the warm water and set aside for 5 to 10 minutes, or until bubbles start to form.

When the yeast is bubbly, pour it into the dry ingredients, add the remaining wet ingredients and stir to combine.

Divide the dough in half and place each half onto the prepared baking sheets. With wet hands, shape into focaccia shapes of about 10 x 12 inches, and 2 inches thick.

Drizzle each loaf with olive oil and scatter over extra herbs and sea salt. Press the sliced tomatoes into the top. Cover the dough in plastic wrap and let it rise in a warm place for about 30 minutes, until it has doubled in size. Once the bread has increased in size, remove the plastic wrap and plunge your fingers into the dough to make small indentations in the top and drizzle with olive oil.

Preheat the oven to 375°F. Bake for around 30 minutes, drizzling the bread with extra olive oil around halfway through the cooking time. Remove from the oven and transfer to a wire rack to cool.

# SWEET POTATO CORNBREAD

Unlike the more savory version, often made with herbs or chiles, the sweet potato in my cornbread makes this dish naturally sweeter. It makes a great companion for chili or black-eyed peas. But I could easily eat a pan full in one sitting with just butter and honey.

## SERVES 2 TO 4

1 large sweet potato, peeled

1¼ cups fine cornmeal or polenta

1¼ cups gluten-free all-purpose flour (I use Cup4Cup)

½ teaspoon baking soda

2 teaspoons gluten-free baking powder

1 teaspoon sea salt

½ cup olive oil

½ cup unsweetened almond milk or dairy milk

½ cup light brown sugar

3 free-range eggs

1 teaspoon vanilla extract

sunflower or canola oil, for greasing

Preheat the oven to 425°F.

Cut the sweet potato into chunks and cook in a large saucepan of salted water for 10 to 15 minutes, or until tender. Drain well and either mash or purée.

Combine the cornmeal, flour, baking soda, baking powder, and salt in a large bowl.

In a jug, combine the olive oil, milk, brown sugar, eggs, and vanilla and lightly whisk to combine.

Add the wet mixture to the dry ingredients and combine. Mix in the sweet potato purée.

Brush a 10-inch cast-iron pan with sunflower or canola oil and place in the hot oven. Remove when hot (be careful and use an oven mitt) and add the mixture to pan, making sure it is even, smoothing it out on the top. Return the pan to the hot oven and cook for 18 to 20 minutes, or until the cornbread is golden and firm to the touch. Serve either warm, directly from the pan, or cool: either way is sooo good.

# IRISH SODA BREAD

Soda bread is a traditional Irish bread that uses baking soda, rather than yeast. In Ireland and in the UK, soda bread is usually a savory brown bread, but in the US, we have a different interpretation. So to avoid any doubt, I have named this Fruit Soda Bread so there are no surprises for any aficionados out there!

My version is filled with orange and currants and is sweet, rather than savory. It's the perfect accompaniment for a cup of tea or coffee.

## MAKES 1 LOAF

- ½ cup oat flour, plus extra for dusting
- ½ cup millet flour
- ½ cup potato starch
- ½ cup sorghum flour
- 2 tablespoons light brown sugar
- 1½ teaspoons gluten-free baking powder
- 1 teaspoon baking soda
- 1 teaspoon sea salt
- 2 teaspoons xanthan gum
- 5 tablespoons unsalted butter, chopped and chilled
- ¾ cup milk (or non-dairy milk of choice)
- 2 free-range eggs
- 1 teaspoon orange juice
- 2 teaspoons orange zest
- 1 tablespoon honey
- 1 cup currants or raisins

Preheat the oven to 400°F.

Dust a baking sheet with oat flour.

In a large bowl, combine the flours, brown sugar, baking powder, baking soda, salt, and xanthan gum and mix to combine. Add the butter and, using your fingertips, rub into the dry ingredients until evenly dispersed and the mixture resembles coarse breadcrumbs.

In a separate bowl, whisk the milk, eggs, orange juice, and zest and honey together. Make a well in the center of the dry mixture and add the wet ingredients. Gently mix, using a silicone or rubber spatula until a sticky dough forms. Gently mix in the currants or raisins.

Shape into a round loaf about 8 inches in diameter, dust with oat flour and place on the dusted baking sheet. Using a sharp knife, cut the signature crisscross into the dough. Bake for 35 to 40 minutes until the loaf is golden and firm to the touch and a toothpick or cake tester comes out clean.

Serve warm (and a bit crumbly) or cool completely for a firmer loaf. This bread is amazing the next day, sliced and toasted and topped with butter.

# ROSEMARY FARINATA

In Genoa this unleavened bread is called *farinata*. In Tuscany it's *cecina*, in Nice it's *socca*. What is agreed on by everyone is that it's super easy to make from chickpea flour. I love it with fresh rosemary, the traditional Italian way, but in North Africa they add cumin, and in India it's made with green chiles and onions. Once you've made this once you can adapt it to sit alongside so many dishes; it's a fail-safe flatbread. It also works really well with an aperitif.

## MAKES 2

1½ cups chickpea flour (the best type for this dish is gram flour)

1 teaspoon gluten-free baking powder

1 teaspoon sea salt, plus extra to serve

4 tablespoons extra virgin olive oil, plus extra for drizzling

1 tablespoon coarsely chopped rosemary

Preheat the oven to 425°F.

Combine the flour, baking powder, and salt in a mixing bowl. Add 2 tablespoons of the olive oil and 1 cup of water and whisk until smooth—it will have the consistency of pancake batter. Leave to rest for at least 20 minutes (or up to 1 hour), skimming off any froth that forms on the surface.

Heat an 8- to 9-inch heavy-based, ovenproof frying pan over a medium heat. Add the remaining olive oil and, when the oil starts to shimmer, pour in half the batter. Sprinkle half the chopped rosemary over the batter and cook, until bubbling and it looks set around the edges.

Transfer the pan to the oven and cook for 7 to 10 minutes or until golden and crisp at the edges and set in the center. Turn the farinata out onto a board, sprinkle with a little sea salt and drizzle with extra virgin olive oil. Repeat with the remaining batter.

Cut into slices and serve warm.

# BRIOCHE

One of the most devastating prospects of going gluten free for me was the loss of bread, and particularly the eggy and sweet brioche, toasted and spread with butter or dipped in egg and then fried as French toast. So many sublime textures and flavors that I had taken for granted my whole life were now suddenly gone. People may say that woman cannot live by bread alone, but for me, brioche was an essential component to my life.

I definitely had some poor results while trying to perfect my gluten-free brioche—some early attempts were completely inedible. But once I had learned more about all the new flours I was using, I finally worked it out, so luckily, you can now make the brilliant brioche your friend once again. You can freeze this for up to 2 months.

## MAKES 12

¾ cup white rice flour

⅓ cup cornstarch

⅓ cup brown rice flour

½ cup tapioca flour

½ cup potato flour

1½ teaspoons xanthan gum

½ teaspoon sea salt

2 tablespoons superfine sugar

1 packet instant yeast (such as Red Star)

1½ sticks chilled unsalted butter, cut into small cubes

¾ cup milk, plus 1 tablespoon for egg wash

1 tablespoon honey

2 large free-range eggs, beaten, plus 1 extra for egg wash

---

Grease 12 individual brioche tins.

Combine the flours, xanthan gum, salt, sugar, and yeast in a large mixing bowl. Add the chilled butter and rub into the mix with your fingertips until it forms small pieces (about the size of a pea); do not overwork the butter into the mixture.

Warm the milk and honey in a small saucepan until tepid. Add the milk and the eggs to the flour mixture and mix with a large metal spoon, until combined. This will be quite a wet mixture—more like a cake batter—but this is fine … don't panic!

Spoon the mixture into the prepared brioche tins and smooth the tops. Cover with plastic wrap and leave to rise in a warm place for 1½–2 hours (the dough will rise by about a third).

Preheat the oven to 400°F.

Mix the extra egg with the tablespoon of milk and brush the tops of the brioche with the egg wash. Bake for 12 to 15 minutes, or until darkly golden and risen. Remove from the oven and leave to cool in the tins for at least 5 minutes before turning out onto a wire rack to cool completely. Eat warm or toasted.

# PUFF
# PASTRY

There is a reason why puff pastry has endured for centuries and is used all over the world—because it's just so darned tasty. I am not going to lie though—this is not for the faint-hearted or anyone in a rush. You will need a long evening or a weekend to do it. However, there is something incredibly satisfying about making your own puff pastry, especially when it's gluten-free.

This recipe forms two blocks, but you can make more in one go and simply freeze the extra blocks for later use.

The basic premise for puff pastry is all about making packets—one of dough (called *détrempe*) and one of butter (called *beurrage*)—and an envelope, then placing one inside the other, folding and rolling to create gaps, i.e. what creates the puff. It may seem daunting the first time you do this, but it does get easier, I promise.

## MAKES 2 BLOCKS

### FOR THE DOUGH PACKET (*DÉTREMPE*)

¾ cup potato starch

½ cup plus 2 tablespoons tapioca starch

¼ cup expandex (see note on page 184)

½ cup superfine sorghum flour

½ cup brown rice flour

½ cup sweet rice flour, plus extra for rolling

1 teaspoon xanthan gum

1 teaspoon sea salt

2 tablespoons powdered milk

1 stick (½ cup) unsalted butter, cold

¾ cup chilled water

### FOR THE BUTTER PACKET (*BEURRAGE*)

1 tablespoon superfine sweet rice flour/glutinous rice flour, plus extra for dusting

1 stick (½ cup) unsalted butter, chilled

Begin with the dough packet (*détrempe*). Sift the and flours for the dough packet into a large bowl. Add the xanthan gum, salt, and powdered milk. Using your fingertips, rub the chilled butter into the flour mixture until it resembles coarse breadcrumbs.

Using a large spoon or flat-bladed knife, stir in enough of the chilled water to make the pastry come together in clumps—it should stick together. If there is any dry flour left in the bowl, you may need to add a little extra water.

Knead the dough for 5 minutes until it is elastic and smooth and only cracks slightly when folded over itself. Shape into a square, wrap in plastic wrap and chill in the refrigerator for 15 to 20 minutes.

Meanwhile, prepare the butter packet (*beurrage*). Place a sheet of plastic wrap on the counter and sprinkle with sweet rice flour. Place the butter on top and top with the remaining flour. Cover with another sheet of plastic wrap and, using a rolling pin, first gently press down the butter to flatten and then roll slightly. Remove the top layer of plastic wrap and fold the butter in half onto itself, then repeat by covering the butter again in plastic wrap and flattening again. Repeat 2 or 3 times until the butter is pliable, then shape the butter into four 4-inch squares. Wrap in plastic wrap and chill in the refrigerator for 10 minutes.

*Recipe continues overleaf*

Now for the turns.

Dust a work surface with sweet rice flour (on a Silpat non-stick baking mat if you have one) and also dust your rolling pin.

Roll out the 4 edges of the dough packet, leaving the middle section untouched. Make sure the middle is the same size as the butter packet and the flaps are deep enough to fold over it.

Place the butter packet in the center of the dough packet and cover with the flaps to fully conceal it. This is your first envelope fold.

Gently pat down the area with a rolling pin before rolling it out into a rectangle 3 times as long as it is wide. Then fold the top third over into the middle and the bottom third over to meet and complete the first letter fold.

Turn 90 degrees and repeat the letter fold twice. Wrap and chill in the refrigerator for 1 hour.

Repeat with two more turns and chill again for 1 hour.

Repeat the final 2 turns and chill for at least 2 hours or overnight before using.

You can freeze the puff pastry and simply thaw and use for instance, for my Salmon Wellington (see page 76).

## INGREDIENT NOTE

*Expandex is a gluten-free starch made from modified tapioca starch and is used to lighten the texture of baked goods, especially with flours like sorghum and buckwheat, to help give flexibility and elasticity to doughs. It is especially useful to help roll doughs like puff pastry, making them more pliable. It also gives expansion to breads, improving their softness and texture.*

# GARLIC CROUTONS

Soups, salads, stews—in fact, anything that demands a little extra something—might need a handful of croutons. Obviously, you can buy these, but I have to say, not only are homemade croutons so much tastier, they also won't have the preservatives and flavor enhancers you find in a lot of the store-bought versions. I use garlic and thyme in mine, but you can adapt the herbs to suit the dish or your personal taste. I make a batch to go with my soups, but they are perfect for green salads too, for an extra bit of bite.

## SERVES 4

1 loaf of day-old white gluten-free bread

3 garlic cloves, crushed

1 tablespoon chopped thyme leaves (optional)

4 tablespoons olive oil

sea salt and freshly ground black pepper

Preheat the oven to 400°F.

Line a large baking sheet with parchment paper.

Cut the loaf into eight ½-inch thick slices. Remove the crusts from the bread and cut into ½-inch cubes.

Place the bread cubes in a large bowl and sprinkle with garlic and thyme, if using, and pour over the oil. Toss well to coat.

Transfer the bread cubes, in a single layer, to the prepared baking sheet and season with a little salt and black pepper.

Bake for 10 to 15 minutes, tossing occasionally, or until browned and crisp. Leave to cool on the sheet. You can store the croutons in an airtight container for up to 2 days.

## TIP

*For even color and crispness, remember to shake the pan regularly while the croutons are cooking, and keep an eye on them to make sure they don't burn.*

# CORN TORTILLAS

Corn tortillas are naturally gluten free. I have tried making flour tortillas gluten free, but they never really worked for me, so I thought: why fight it, when these are a fabulous alternative, just as tasty and even more authentic? It's the simplest of recipes, and you can also add a little teaspoon of fresh lime juice to the water for a slightly different flavor. These are the perfect accompaniment to any Mexican dish.

## MAKES 12

1 cup masa harina

pinch of coarse sea salt

¾ cup plus 2 tablespoons cold water

1 teaspoon fresh lime juice (optional)

Mix the flour and salt in a bowl and slowly add the water until it forms a dough. If it's too wet, you can just add some more flour; equally, if it's looking too dry, add some more water. The dough shouldn't crack around the edges when you press it between your palms before rolling (if it does, you need to add a little more water).

Divide the dough into 12 balls for large tortillas (you can make smaller tortillas if you wish; just divide into 20 balls). Flatten with a tortilla press or by sandwiching the dough between 2 pieces of plastic wrap, then roll out really thinly with a rolling pin, so each tortilla is around 5 inches in diameter and about the thickness of a dime.

Heat a griddle pan over a high heat and cook the tortillas on each side for 1 to 1½ minutes until lightly colored. Wrap them in a dishtowel to retain the moisture. You can keep these for a couple of days, but personally, I prefer my tortillas warm and fresh every time!

## TIP

*For the best gluten-free tortillas you should always use masa harina, which can be found in most grocery stores and online.*

# RESOURCES

## GLUTEN-FREE BRANDS

Sometimes store-bought is so much easier—my favorite gluten-free brands all produce some great foods that are my go-to choices for easy and tasty options—either as standalones or as part of ingredients lists.

Whole Foods is my go-to store in NYC and also in London, as it has the best and most exhaustive range of gluten-free products. I also am a huge fan of Dean and Deluca and Williams-Sonoma. I go to the Union Square farmer's market for fresh vegetables and fruit. My favorite Gluten Free general flour mixes are Cup4Cup and Pamela's. I use a lot of Bob's Red Mill products—from gums and starches to rice flours. In the UK I use Dove's Farm Gluten Free Flour (Plain and/or Self Raising). I use a lot of quinoa products—including Andean Dream quinoa pastas. For pastas I use Jovial, Ancient Harvest, and Rummo. Sometimes we need to grab something ready-made—I go for frozen breads. Schar is a good all round European brand—I always buy their gram crackers and their Lady Fingers biscuits for desserts. Blue Diamond's Artisan Nut-thins are great and come in Chia, Flax, and Sesame seed varieties. If I want a pre-made pie crust I opt for Whole Foods Market Bakehouse pie shells.

My favorite gluten-free bakery is Helmut Newcake in Paris and also Beyond Bread in London. The best gluten-free pizza restaurants are hands-down found in NYC (sorry London!); Emporio, Kesté, Rubi Rosa and Sensa Gluten are my top choices. Cafe Gratitude and Urth Caffe in LA—well known but oh-so-good. Siggy's have the best gluten-free burgers as do Bareburger and Shake Shack, also in NYC. Nourish Kitchen and of course Butcher's Daughter are also two old favorites of mine.

## MY SUPER FOOD SUPER HEROES

Everyone has their own list of the foods that make their gut go crazy with delight. From vinegars to coconuts, they all help pack a punch with the food choices we make. Here is a list of my personal super heroes—ingredients that I try to include daily or weekly: Açaí, Bee pollen, Coconut water, Coconut flakes, Coconut oil, Coconut yogurt, Greek yogurt, Goji berries, Raw cacao, Maca, Spirulina, Matcha, Red bell peppers, Chia seeds, Kale, Pumpkin seeds, Blueberries, Quinoa, Tamari.

For my detailed flour glossary, see pages 14 to 17.

## MY KITCHEN GADGETS

Of course my Vitamix is my dearest partner—for soups, smoothies, and remedies. I use a Kuvings Juicer—it's cold-pressed for the best results. I use a Cuisinart Food Processor and a KitchenAid mixer, ice-cream, and yogurt maker. I must admit I am an supplement fan—Omega 3 and probiotics especially—and for my personal regime one of my most loved products is The Beauty Chef Glow probiotic powder.

I have talked at length about the electrical tools I use in the book, however I would be at a complete loss without my Imperia pasta machine and my Waring Pro belgian waffle maker—and last but not least I got my vintage cast iron tortilla press from eBay for just $15!

# INDEX

# ACKNOWLEDGMENTS

There are so many people that helped make my dream of writing a book into reality. Firstly, to Alan, who made this book, and everything, possible. You gave me the push I needed to start writing and supported me along the way, trying every one of the endless recipes I put in front of you and always giving your honest opinion.

Thank you to Antonia and Martin Deeson at Deeson & Deeson for guiding me through this journey, to my agent Charlie Brotherstone, my US publicist and best friend Akbar Hamid and his team at The 5th Column, and Dirk Singer and Lea Rice for all their help. Stephen, Sanga, Richard, and Valerie for being there for me.

Thank you to my amazing editor Tara O'Sullivan, photographer Clare Winfield, designer Abi Hartshorne, and styling team of Annie Rigg and Polly Webb-Wilson for helping to create my vision and making it look even more beautiful than I could have imagined. And of course, to Kyle Cathie for believing in this book and to everyone at Octopus.

A huge thank you to Quentin Bacon and Maya Rossi in New York—guys, you gave me the tools to build the brand. Thank you. To David Herbert, Rachel Wood, and Katy Gilhooly. Thank you Rebecca Minkoff for believing in me and supporting me from the start. Thanks to Kris Zero for making me look and feel amazing. Thank you to Lubov Azria for helping me to launch my catering company during New York Fashion Week.

A huge thank you to my Mom for always supporting my love of cooking from childhood onwards and letting me loose in her kitchen—and then cleaning up whatever mess I made. I couldn't have ever pursued cooking and culinary school without the support of my family.

And of course, to my Nana, who I still think of every day, especially when I am cooking. I would also like to send a very special thank you to all my amazing followers—you make me smile and laugh and think about new ways to cook every single day.